Foreword by Rt Hon Robert Halfon MP, former Skills Minister, and Chair of the House of Commons Education Select Committee

D1826226

Bridge That Gap!

How Schools Can Help Students Get Their First Job And Build The Career They Want

Angela Middleton

Bridge That Gap!

First published in 2018 by

Panoma Press Ltd
48 St Vincent Drive, St Albans, Herts, AL1 5SJ, UK
info@panomapress.com
www.panomapress.com

Book layout by Neil Coe.

Printed on acid-free paper from managed forests.

ISBN 978-1-784521-35-6

Printed and bound in Great Britain by
TJ International Ltd, Padstow, Cornwall

Dedication

To my team at MiddletonMurray − past, present and future −
who have worked tirelessly to create and deliver a transformation
programme for thousands of young people which literally takes
them from Zero to Degree and which we have proven can launch
aspirations and a rewarding career for every student in the UK.

Bst Wishs

Angela Middleton

Dec. '18

Acknowledgement

Acknowledging the tremendous efforts of teaching staff around the country who work hard every day at upskilling our young people. Being a global leader with top rates of productivity is not easy, but we will get there!

Foreword

On my frequent visits around England to FE colleges and private education providers to meet with apprentices and students, I have lost count of how many new acquaintances have told me about their poor career advice at school. I have even met higher and degree apprentices who offered to return to their old schools to provide an insight into skills and apprenticeship careers, yet were inexplicably refused.

Millions of pounds are spent by the government on 'big careers organisations', yet the outcomes are often mixed. There is duplication and confusion for all concerned. As *Bridge That Gap!* reminds us, there are still 783,000 16 to 24-year-olds classed as not in work, education or training, despite thousands of vacancies, in all fields from apprenticeships, traineeships, and internships. Clearly, something is going wrong.

If we are to transform the prospects of thousands of pupils and students in our country and ensure we offer a real ladder of opportunity for all – whatever their background or circumstance – we need a radical shake-up of careers advice.

Angela Middleton's book does just that, offering a model that fundamentally rethinks how we prepare young people for the world of work: embedding careers advice in all parts of the curriculum and engaging every stakeholder (from the pupils, parents and teachers, to governors and even Ofsted), in setting career life goals.

This book makes important recommendations to ensure that no pupil is left behind, by suggesting a programme of mentoring – changing negative perspectives before teaching knowledge has even begun. There are thoughtful proposals on making work experience, traineeships and placements an essential part of education, on bringing businesses and alumni on board, and other original ideas, such as encouraging the positive use of social media, particularly LinkedIn. It is a two-part book: first, focusing on what should be done, then, providing the tools to make it happen.

I hope that everyone who is passionate about building careers advice reads *Bridge That Gap!*. I know what Angela Middleton is proposing, works – I have seen it first hand at MiddletonMurray.

Rt Hon Robert Halfon MP is a former Skills Minister, and served in the Cabinet under David Cameron from 2015 to 2016. He is currently Chair of the House of Commons Education Select Committee.

Introduction

In the UK there is a terrifying gap for many students between school and work, the time when a school leaver has left the security of school life but has not yet secured their first job. Whether it lasts for just a few days, a few months or even a few years, this gap causes a tragic loss of confidence and an absence of aspiration in our precious young people, the people who will build our future economy. I am not exaggerating when I say how bad things are right now compared to how they could be.

We see extreme examples of young people so disillusioned that they even want to take their own life; their experiences of school were alienating and the system has failed them. In some areas of the UK there is still a toxic atmosphere in schools and this fosters violence, stabbings, gun crime, drugs, and introduction to gangs and radicalism in the worst cases. Parents and carers are often at their wits' end as they are not equipped to advise and don't know where to go to obtain the information they feel their child needs.

We all need to take responsibility for how badly we are currently preparing students for real life and the negative effect this has not just on the individuals but society as a whole. We *need* to change things and I am laying out in this book a step by step solution to help achieve that. The future of the UK is at stake here, and yet we can resolve so much of this by facilitating true collaboration between schools and employers. This book provides a complete methodology and template for schools to arm their students with the right skills, knowledge, techniques and contacts to build their aspirations and to secure their first jobs before leaving school – ie to bridge that gap altogether.

Why am I qualified to write this book? I believe my experience to date, as summarised below, will help to explain this.

My company has worked with young people for several years, arming them with necessary life and employability skills, introducing them to our employer clients, securing them their first job, and then delivering a five-year apprenticeship – effectively taking them from Zero to Degree which is one of our main brands. In the main, I find these young people come to us 'on the back foot' meaning they have dropped out of school or college or a job that doesn't suit them and are having difficulty getting started on their career ladder. The techniques we have developed and utilise once they join us mean they are very quickly on to that career ladder, we secure them a great job, not just any job, and they are on their way.

We see this work with young people from all walks of life and with all abilities, including those with additional needs, those with a history of youth offending, those from troubled backgrounds, **and** those with very few challenges and with 3 x A* at A level. We can absolutely guarantee our programmes work, and we have thousands of case studies and testimonials to support that. Indeed, I wrote a book providing a step by step guide for young people, which can be read in conjunction with this one, entitled *How To Get Your First Job And Build The Career You Want* knowing that these techniques work and wanting to help as many people as possible.

My involvement with schools: despite the great results we achieve, it is clear to me that if we tackled some of the issues we see before they happened, it would be so much easier and more enjoyable for the young person. In other words, I see a need to tackle the issue of youth unemployment more 'at source' ie before they have left school or college and before they take a course or job that doesn't suit their aspirations. This led me to become more involved in schools and colleges, firstly to find out what goes on in them from a careers preparation perspective, and secondly to see if I could help in this area.

Initially, I offered free talks from myself or my staff to school assemblies, student careers evenings, university careers lessons etc, and later I took up two separate school governor roles in two quite different senior schools. I also encouraged my staff to do the same. We have also delivered many talks about employer engagement and careers development at careers advisor events. Now, it is a key part of the remit of each of my branch managers to fully engage with the schools, colleges and universities in their area to build relationships and to help with free advice wherever they can. We also offer more comprehensive programmes to these organisations on a commercial basis.

I have been personally engaged with many ministers and staff of our Department for Education (DfE) for many years – to provide support and to understand the wider challenges. Most recently, I have launched my 'Limitless Campaign' – a manifesto championing a new strategy that outlines how governments, schools and employers can provide more expedient careers advice and work experience. The manifesto consists of five key pillars: careers advice should be free and accessible to everyone; careers advice should be open to all; careers advice must be delivered by a range of actors more innovatively; careers advice should be modernised to fit the contemporary jobs market; and careers advice should be multifaceted.

This is supported by our own research where 80% of the students we formally surveyed stated that careers advice had failed them. I am looking forward to working on these proposals with schools, employers, and staff from the DfE, and many of the themes at the heart of our campaign are considered here as well.

I have produced a series of podcasts interviewing experts in a variety of professions for their advice on what it is like to do that job and how to achieve the same. This is downloadable for free from iTunes and is a great way for students, teachers, parents and anyone interested in changing careers to access careers information when they want it in an easily accessible format for everyone.

I am a parent myself and have seen first-hand the struggles of my own children and their peers to build aspirational futures for themselves. As an aside, this permeates into later life and I have also seen it amongst clients of MiddletonMurray and personal friends as individuals in later life decide they want to switch careers and change their lives.

Throughout this work, what I have seen is a strong desire on the part of the schools, colleges, universities and the Department for Education to support students in achieving great careers. I've also seen that they have a great thirst for knowledge in order to achieve this. I have often had discussions with head teachers and principals where we have agreed that it would be the panacea if every one of their students, whatever their level, had a fantastic destination all sorted for them before the end of their final term, whether that was the right further or higher education or the right first job and/ or apprenticeship. I know myself that this would be most certainly achievable, even easy, and so I decided to write this second book for school leaders and teaching staff to help them achieve the best long-term outcomes for their students over and above the educational outputs.

My overriding message throughout this book is that this work can be done in school without interrupting academic progress, and indeed it must be done if we are to see our students getting the outcomes they deserve without wasting time in the gap between school and finally starting with an employer.

Just one important acknowledgement: I am not a qualified teacher and I have not worked within a school, so I cannot profess to have encountered all the demands and pressures that teachers work under on a day to day basis. Having said that, I do believe I have some really useful alternative experience to be able to impart some advice to those that are and who do, including the following:

- My company is a private recruitment and training consultancy that trains thousands of young people from 16 through to 24 and sometimes older, on full-time roll on roll off programmes in Maths and English, and a holistic approach to aspirations and employability – usually after they have found themselves unemployed.

- At the time of writing, we have achieved three Ofsted Grade 'Good's, (one for our pre-employment programme, one for our apprenticeship delivery, and most recently one for the two programmes combined) and I understand all the preparation and management that it takes to achieve and sustain this level of quality.

- We have direct government-funded contracts which need rigorous management for compliance and audit, and I understand the necessity for success rates in order to maintain an appropriate level of funding.

- I see the issues, problems and demands that teachers at all levels face first-hand in my school governor roles.

- I have relationships with thousands of employers (both small and large companies) and know how they operate, what they want and how they think.

- I know that our techniques work and are proven.

So in summary, I have seen that educational organisations can have a massive impact on the early careers success of their students and ensure they do not go through any periods of disillusionment, and I want to spread the word on how to achieve this. Sadly I am not able to work on a one-to-one basis with every educational organisation. Therefore, I have written this book in the hope that it will enable our techniques to be utilised as widely as possible across the UK to promote great careers starts for our young people, and in the process make the roles of all educators even more rewarding and fulfilling than they already are, through being able to influence not only their students' education but also their career and ultimately their life as well.

Before you delve into the content of this book, take a look at a very short film produced by the BBC which illustrates many of the points I will make. It illustrates our techniques beautifully and I hope brings to life for the viewer much of what I describe in this book. https://www.youtube.com/watch?v=dzCF8WkkNSk

Contents

Dedication 3

Acknowledgement 4

Foreword 5

Introduction 7

PART 1 – THE PROBLEM AND HOW TO ADDRESS IT 20

Chapter 1 – The Problem: Jobs are Everywhere But So Are NEETs – Why? 21

The Nine Top Issues We See All The Time When Young People Come To Us 23

Lack of vision 23

Lack of self-belief 24

Parents/carers are not aligned 24

Teacher shortage and disillusionment 25

Schools driven by Ofsted gradings and funding rules 26

Qualifications prioritised over outcomes 27

Employers have never been engaged 29

Limited careers advice 30

No alumni 31

Chapter 2 – Overcoming Lack Of Aspiration And Vision: Help Students Build A Compelling Life Plan 33

Questions to ask 34

Creating a positive mindset 38

Aligning life planning to business planning 39

Making it fun but serious – the charter 39

Culture change 40

Tools 42

Success Story 1 43

**Chapter 3 – Overcoming Lack Of Self Belief:
Help Students Build A Step By Step Roadmap
To Achieve Their Vision** **45**

Progression 46

Milestones 47

Overcoming hurdles 47

Tenacity 49

Freedom to change and adapt 50

Integration with stakeholders 51

Teachers 51

Parents 51

Funders and inspectorate 52

Leadership team and governors 52

Local authority and alumni manager 53

Success Story 2 54

**Chapter 4 – Aligning The Student Life Plan
With Parent/Carer Goals** **57**

Parent/carer requirements 58

Parent/carer issues 59

Parent/carer time restraints   60

Parent/carer unique support   62

The school and parent/carer charter   62

Success Story 3   63

Chapter 5 – Aligning The Student Life Plan With School Leadership, Teacher And Governor Goals   65

What teachers want   65

Life plan for the school   66

What governors want   66

Teacher life planning   67

Succession planning for the school   70

Teaching and learning grades   70

Success Story 4   71

Chapter 6 – Aligning The Student Life Plan With Ofsted And Funder Goals   73

Focus on outcomes   74

Alumni tracking   75

Alignment   75

Teaching and learning   76

Parents and Ofsted   78

Parent and governor support   79

School alumni support   79

Success Story 5   80

Chapter 7 – Aligning The Student Life Plan With The Curriculum And Exam Goals 81

Concept of product and packaging 81

Planning the curriculum milestones 82

Overlaying the life plan milestones 83

Cross-referencing academic and life goals 83

The concept of balance 85

Holidays 86

Timetabling and turning goals into accomplishments 86

Ongoing Success Story 6 87

Chapter 8 – The Employability Programme: Aligning The Student Life Plan With Employer Requirements And Engaging With Employers 89

What employers want 89

Identifying employer role models 92

Identifying future job opportunities 94

Building relationships between schools and employers 94

Industry sessions 95

Employer taster days 95

Work experience placements 96

First refusal for jobs 97

The hidden job market 97

Studying job advertisements 98

CV writing 99

30-second elevator pitch training   99

Interview training   100

Mock interviews with employers   100

Enhancing the life plan   101

Finding job opportunities for your students   101

Repeating and refining the employability programme   102

Staying connected with employers   102

What schools can offer employers   102

Success Story 7   103

Chapter 9 – Resourcing The Employability Programme: How To Get Maximum Benefit From Careers Advisors   105

Sourcing careers advisors   105

Selection process for a careers advisor   106

Employer links   106

Industry knowledge   106

Knowledge of career options   107

Ofsted and other ratings   107

Funding   107

Motivation and innovation   108

Time available   108

Resources available   108

Location	109
Ability to influence	109
Funding and cost	109
How to manage the advisor	110
Growing your own	110
Examples of good practice	111
Success Story 8	111

Chapter 10 – Maintaining An Active Alumni To Achieve Repeat Placements And Obtain Case Studies

Chapter 10 – Maintaining An Active Alumni To Achieve Repeat Placements And Obtain Case Studies	**113**
Ex-students	113
Ex-parents	114
Ex-teachers	114
Ex-governors	115
Inspectorates and other authorities	115
Past employers	115
Suppliers	116
Ways to stay engaged with alumni	116
Managing the exit process	116
Database marketing	117
Awards events	118
Success Story 9	119

PART 2 – ACTIONABLE TOOLS AND TEMPLATES 122

The MiddletonMurray Traineeship Scheme of Works   123

Employability and Life Planning   124

Life Planning – Personal Branding   128

Employability – Social Media   132

Customer Service   136

You and the World of Work   141

Project Work   145

Five Year Goals   148

Life Plan Template   152

Life Plan   154

Niche template/sectors of work   158

Purpose of a CV   166

Content of your CV   166

Summary   167

Skills and qualifications   167

Work experience and key achievements   167

Other points regarding content   167

Length of your CV   168

Covering letter   171

Covering letter template   172

Application forms   173

Emails and voicemails   173

    Your email address   173

    Your emails   174

    Your voicemails   174

Social media   175

    Be careful!   175

    Facebook   176

    Your profile picture   177

    LinkedIn   177

    Twitter   178

    Instagram   179

    Video (YouTube)   179

Interview questions to practise   181

Questions you might be asked   185

    Competency questions   185

    Scenario questions   185

    Questions about you   186

Podcast Resources on iTunes – Angela Middleton's
'iwant2ba'   187

Apprentice of the Month   189

Example school success stories   190

About The Author   192

Part 1

THE PROBLEM AND HOW TO ADDRESS IT

Chapter 1

The Problem:
Jobs are Everywhere
But So Are NEETs – Why?

Youth unemployment remains a major issue for the UK today. In 2018 it was reported that 783,000 people aged 16-24 were Not in Education, Employment or Training (NEET), representing 11.2% of the age group and an upward trend from the previous quarter whilst the unemployment rate (the proportion of the economically active population who are unemployed) for 16-24-year-olds was 37% (Source: House of Commons Library Briefing Paper Numbers 5871 and 6705). This is despite us officially coming out of recession, and despite the various initiatives implemented by the government, such as raising the age of education participation to 18, introducing apprenticeship schemes and incentives, and encouraging small businesses to participate with work experience initiatives and larger businesses to pay an apprenticeship levy.

It is also despite the fact that there is no shortage of first jobs for these young people. At the time of writing there are 21,000 apprenticeship vacancies on the UK.gov website with thousands being added weekly, and on LinkedIn today there are 9,000 apprenticeship vacancies, 13,000 trainee vacancies and 1,000 internships. That's just the jobs advertised. It excludes what we call the 'hidden jobs market' – those vacancies that exist or could exist if we just ask and yet they are not advertised.

So this is the issue. We have jobs, we have skills shortages and yet we have school leavers without jobs.

In my business, which specialises in placing young people into their first job, we are always surprised to have this strange conundrum whereby we have numerous open vacancies for first jobs and numerous young applicants to fill them and yet they are not suitable for each other. We find we have to do a tremendous amount of work with the young people before we can put them forward for the vacancies we have, and often that they fail the interviews, or if they pass them, don't manage to retain the job once they have secured it. We see a lack of direction and commitment on the part of the young person and a general apathy for wanting to build a career. It often amazes us that after saying they will do anything to get a job, when they do get one they quickly become disillusioned and drop out. Why is this?

We have seen that there are a number of reasons which stem from some things that have not happened while they were still at school. We find that once we address these things we can completely turn them around and set them on a great career path. It always strikes me that it is such a shame we get these youngsters coming to us so much 'on the back foot'; often they have had a job but didn't like it or they have dropped out of college. They feel disillusioned and we have to spend a lot of time building them back up before we can place them.

What we do is not rocket science though, and if our techniques were used in school they wouldn't have to go through this period of disillusionment and could go straight into great jobs, bypassing organisations such as mine. Not only that but these simple techniques compel them to learn, and therefore if they were applied in school I believe academic grades and attendance would dramatically increase in schools too.

I would like to see a situation where the whole of a leaving year are clear on their destination before they leave school, where they all have either university places to go to or apprenticeships with great employers. We do not want our young people leaving school and entering colleges to do courses that are simply a 'fall back' position for them. We want our young people to use their school time as the fantastic stepping stone it is – into a great career and beyond. This book outlines what the issues are and then addresses them one by one. I hope as a school professional you will enjoy the book and be able to utilise its contents to make your school a more productive and enjoyable experience, not only for the student but for you, your colleagues and the parent/carer, and that together we are able to achieve the great destination results that we all aspire to.

The Nine Top Issues We See All The Time When Young People Come To Us

Lack of vision

We see young people leaving school with little or no vision of what they want to do. We frequently hear that they have 'tried everything' to get a job and will 'do any job' when the reality is quite the opposite. It is this lack of direction that causes them to take a scattergun approach to job hunting with the resulting poor results. We see that where careers advice in schools has taken place it often bears little if any relation to a 'Life Vision' – meaning there is a disconnect between what the young person really wants for their life and what they think they might get from a career. No one has sat that young person down and asked them what they want their life to be like in ten years' time before then discussing careers that might make that vision become a reality.

Similarly, because there is such a lack of focus in schools on what the student wants for their life, we often hear that the student didn't like school. I believe this is often because they didn't see the relevance of school to a career and ultimately a life vision. They often don't see school as the critical stepping stone it is and instead view it as an interim distraction before they can start their first job.

If they were to see this connection they would have a greater desire to obtain the necessary qualifications, and hence achieve better grades. Attendance improves too when they understand why they are there.

Lack of self-belief

Youngsters leave school doubting their own abilities and unclear on how to achieve even the most general plans. They have no roadmap to achieving their goals even if they are clear on what those goals are – which generally they are not. Instead they might focus on celebrity lifestyles and achievements without realising that celebrities achieve what they do due to hard work that undoubtedly goes into anyone becoming a celebrity! I did a school assembly talk recently and encountered a lot of excitement when I told them about a celebrity friend of mine. What they didn't know was anything about this person's history and how hard they had worked for years to get where they were.

These stories are not the ones that get highlighted in the press, and I found it interesting that the youngsters did not appreciate this aspect of the celebrity they thought they knew so well. They have an acceptance that they cannot achieve such lofty heights and actually write themselves off at a very young age. There is a general acceptance of limitations even at this age. We often meet 17-year-olds who now wish they had worked harder at school and don't believe that they can change everything around and be anything they want. They don't have any understanding of milestones or roadmapping, or that the world is actually their oyster at this tender age. They are unaware that anything can be turned around and anything achieved.

Parents/carers are not aligned

We often see that parents/carers are not involved or engaged in any sort of life plan. Many parents/carers see it as the school's 'job' to motivate, inspire and even entertain their children. When parents/

carers and teachers meet it is to discuss the child's academic progress, and as such there is no aligned plan between these two critical supporters of that child regarding how they are going to get the best career outcome for that child ultimately. Discussions are sometimes short term, focusing on the next academic year. Admittedly, the older the student is, the less appropriate they may feel it is to have their parent/carer involved; however, we find this issue is exacerbated by the fact that careers advice is often given just to the young person and not to the parent/carer.

We often see examples where there have been careers talks and the parent/carer was unaware as they were not invited or encouraged to come along and get involved. Employers are sometimes invited into schools and yet the fact that parents/carers are very often employers themselves seems to be missed. If discipline is an issue, particularly over things like uniform, timekeeping and homework, we see that parents/carers are sometimes in support of their children, defending their poor behaviour rather than supporting the school staff, or even seeing various disciplinary issues as irrelevant.

It is often these things that are most important early on in the workplace though, where poor behaviour is just not tolerated and can easily end in dismissal! Parents/carers are fully aware of this and yet this aspect is not discussed with them and so they may believe the school is being petty or bloody-minded rather than being utilised to back up the school message. I actually see parents/carers being very interested if they are invited to participate, particularly if they are asked to tell the children about their own careers.

Teacher shortage and disillusionment

We know that teachers are a scarce resource and that funding is tight. This often means that teachers themselves can become overworked and therefore have little time to work with youngsters on their life vision and career plan. What's more, teachers are driven to achieve levels of academic progress and good grades; they are not driven to support the teaching and learning of employability skills or to secure job outcomes. Unfortunately, this can result in a downward spiral of disillusionment in the student, frustration in the teacher, more absence from pupils, poor grades, poor behaviour, more stress on the teacher, and maybe in the end more absence from the teacher and thus creating a negative cycle.

If we could find a way that the teachers could be allowed to engage with the students' life plans and life vision, and demonstrate how what they are teaching will fit within that, then we can break the negative cycle. In this way, the students will feel more compelled to learn, whether they enjoy the subject or not, because it is something they need to achieve their bigger picture. It is a means to an end. If that happens, then the teacher will have less issue with discipline and non-attendance (we've witnessed this in our own experience time and time again). This means that the teacher has a greater chance of achieving high success rates, which will not only fulfil the school's goals but also facilitate that teacher achieving his or her own career goals through promotions, higher pay, and hence the achievement of their own life plan too.

Schools driven by Ofsted gradings and funding rules

As we know, what gets measured gets done. Currently Ofsted measures effectiveness of leadership and management, quality of teaching, learning and assessment, and outcomes for students in the context of exam grades and levels of progression rather than job outcomes. Personal development, behaviour and welfare is also now measured as a separate category, but not in terms of job outcomes. Obviously schools are driven to achieve excellence and have a huge amount of work to do, leaving little time for things that are not measured.

Of course leadership and management are strengthened if the big picture for students can be shared, but in reality most schools focus on getting the tangibles that are measured – and jobs is not one of these. As such we see schools fully focused on past, present and future success rates, numbers of levels of progress, closing the gap between advantaged and disadvantaged children, and ways and means to enhance these.

Observations and CPD cycles are rigorously implemented in the best schools with great success and this is a demanding and all-consuming process. What seems to be missing though is the non-educational aspect of compelling the student to learn. If right at the beginning of their time at the school the students were supported to create a clear vision of what they wanted to achieve with their life, and had documented a roadmap to achieving those goals which included the achievement of certain exam grades, they would actually be more compelled to learn.

With this in place, improvements of grades would be the aim of all parties and not just the teachers. Students would know why they had to achieve a good pass in maths GCSE for example, and would come to see and accept that the fact that they might not enjoy it was largely irrelevant. A bit like taking medicine, they would be willing to just get through the learning quickly and diligently in order to achieve the outcome they needed. This in turn would be observed by Ofsted as positive in all areas: leadership, teaching and learning, *and* outcomes for students.

Qualifications prioritised over outcomes

We see youngsters leaving school without appropriate qualifications in maths and English because they did not enjoy these subjects and saw no relevance in having them. They maybe didn't like the teacher of those particular subjects and do not grasp that this is actually quite irrelevant and that maths and English qualifications are not nice to haves but are essentials. They say things like they are no good at maths, and in saying this write themselves off. When they come to us, this mindset takes a lot of undoing as they may have already selected a persona that doesn't care about changing this, as a defence mechanism. They just do not connect the importance of these to their life vision.

On the other hand, we find they have often achieved a cluster of alternative qualifications instead, and with decent grades, but are disappointed because they have found that these qualifications, although enjoyable, are not enough to secure them the job and career they want. Often they have selected these qualifications because they liked the teacher, or their friend had selected it. Sometimes they just don't know why they selected a subject, or they don't care, and they explain that they have never believed that the things they do at school are relevant to the job they want to do. They believe that other qualities will enable them to achieve their goals (back to the celebrity scenario). Sometimes their goals are to achieve significance in their current world because they have never thought about their future environment, and significance is achieved by behaviours other than doing well at school and may even include being the poorest performer at school or the one who does not care.

What is really frustrating is when they emerge with high grades in these qualifications and a grade D in maths or English. They are clearly able to achieve the necessary C grades or equivalent, but because of that lack of life vision and hence motivation, they haven't.

Addressing this issue is totally possible – I know because every day we manage to get young people through their qualification after just a few weeks when they haven't been able to achieve it in two years at school. The answer is to get them to build a life vision they really want to achieve, and then work with them so they understand what they need and why, in order to achieve this vision. Where this involves the achievement of a qualification, we see that they then become compelled to learn quickly and effectively, and they pass the exams. For cases where they dislike the teacher we are extremely direct. We let them know that our own teachers are not entertainers, they are educators, and although supportive, are there to help them achieve what they need to in the life plan. That's it, nothing more.

Of course, we do provide more (we aim to be role models, cheerleaders and mentors, and the testimonials we receive are evidence of this), but we do not communicate that intention to our students! We find students often come to us with this whole 'entertain me' persona. We soon let them know that, unfortunately, this just does not happen in the real world. It's all about what they can offer to the employer and not the other way around which will get them what they ultimately want. This is usually enough to get them to focus and achieve.

Employers have never been engaged

We always present the employer as the 'audience' or the 'buyer' in an interview scenario. The employers are the ones who need to want the young people on their team – and yet we see so often that the young person has never met employers while at school! There has been no relationship building between the school and even the most local businesses, so opportunities for work experience have been limited. Unfortunately, this can also lead to some misconceptions with the students. For example, if they haven't been made aware that they are a commodity that the employer is buying, they can sometimes believe that their CV should be all about what they are looking for rather than what they can offer. It can almost seem that they believe the employer owes them something.

We are often challenged, for example, on why the minimum apprenticeship starting wage is so low. The answer is all about value added. We teach students that the value being offered by them is limited, ie a willingness to learn, whilst the value being added by the employer at the beginning is an opportunity to learn, gain experience *and* get some form of payment. Employment is a value bargain and we work hard to teach that to students very quickly.

Also, through having such little involvement with employers, we find that the young person has no idea of a career niche they might prefer. Hence they have the view that they will try anything and will not realise that this is very off-putting to an employer who is seeking someone with drive and ambition to do just the job he or she is offering. The interesting thing is that employers are often very keen to build relationships with their local schools but have no opportunities to do so and do not know how to approach the schools or how to engage with them. By offering them opportunities to come and do assemblies, talks at careers events, Dragons' Den type competitions, taster days etc, the school can forge these relationships and lay the foundations for future career options for their students.

Limited careers advice

Schools sometimes have a careers advisory function and sometimes it is absolutely great and effective. More often, however, it is old-fashioned and sparse. With limited funds and packed timetables, it is difficult for schools to find the time and expertise to be able to discuss and create life plans with visions with the students and their parent/carer, and hence not much more than a cursory reference is made to careers advice in many schools. We still also see that girls and boys are directed into typical roles for their gender and are not encouraged to look at non-gender typical roles.

Government-funded careers services tend to be hit and miss. Often a careers advisor is allocated a huge caseload of schools and barely gets a chance to meet the students more than once. Schools may therefore decide to pay for private careers advisors. Generally speaking, these will have more time because they are being paid for it, but they will never guarantee outcomes in terms of jobs or even short-term work placements.

No alumni

Schools aren't expected to track their alumni beyond a few months after leaving, and as such they do not keep tabs as their youngsters rise up the ranks of employment. They don't usually have a robust schedule of visiting ex-pupil speakers, and because they don't engage with their alumni they aren't able to draw on contacts to secure work experience placements and even job offers. Case studies of students who have gone on to achieve great careers are consequently difficult for schools to obtain too. All schools will have a rich source of new employment opportunities for their pending leavers; they just need to connect with that source very early on and then maintain active dialogue with the leavers to forge a mature and mutually beneficial relationship that will also benefit their new leavers.

Chapter 2

Overcoming Lack Of Aspiration And Vision: Help Students Build A Compelling Life Plan

The truth is that we all need to feel progress to feel happy, and in order to measure progress we need to have a goal or a benchmark. When children first join a school, just as when adults start a first job, there is a 'honeymoon' period where everything is new and even exciting. The excitement can soon wear off unless something happens during that period to maintain it. With a job, if it does wear off, and the expectations are not met, the adult can soon become disillusioned and this leads to them not doing their best work. The next step from that is that they look for another job and leave, or are asked to leave. However, if this happens to a young person at school, the outcome is not quite as straightforward. It is not such an easy process for young people to change schools as it is jobs and so a negative cycle can be set off at this stage.

On the plus side of this is the fact that, unlike an employer, the school has a 'captive' audience for a definite period of time, so as long as the engagement is there on the part of the young person, they can map out exactly what can be achieved during that time. The key word here is engagement. We have seen that once we have an engaged group of young people we can do wonders with them in a little over six weeks. They turn from unconfident, disillusioned and sometimes angry individuals into the opposite, who can shine at interviews and sustain great jobs. Before they are engaged though, we are wasting our time, so this is something that we work very hard on with great success.

I know that schools experience the same, otherwise why would the same school achieve high rates of progress with one group of students and lower rates of progress with others in relation to their starting ability? It is all relative to their abilities so it isn't due to ability. In my opinion, it is down to engagement and that is what I want to discuss in this chapter.

Schools can make a choice very early on regarding how committed they are to having a 100% engaged captive audience. If they are totally focused on this, and achieve increased engagement with all levels of students, then results will skyrocket. It is therefore well worth the effort of spending considerable time on this right at the beginning in year 7 and then reinforcing it year on year rather than diving into learning.

At my company we are totally non-selective and so we take on many young people with very few grades and a low expectation of their own abilities, and certainly a dislike for learning and certain subjects. We find that within six weeks though we can completely turn this around and get them to achieve an equivalent to Grade C GCSE. This is done by engagement and compelling them to learn before we even start to teach anything. We spend around two of the four weeks on this and it is what gets us the results.

So what does this incorporate? It's a number of things as follows:

Questions to ask

Firstly we ask them to consider why they are here. Their immediate responses are ones we would expect such as 'to get a job', but we ask them why that is. This leads to various responses such as 'to earn money'. Again we ask why. This leads on to responses like 'to have a nice life'. It's at this point that we work with them to describe what that 'nice life' looks like. We get them working in groups and in pairs, we ask lots of questions, and ultimately they end up with a vision board of that life they want for themselves. As part of the process we ask them to relax, close their eyes, and ask themselves lots of questions and write down the answers. We get them to imagine that they are living that life they describe in ten years' time. We ask them to describe the person they can see (them). Questions include:

- How do you look?

- How are you feeling?

- What are you wearing?

- Where are you?

- Where do you live?

- What's your home like?

- Describe it

- Who lives there with you?

- Do you have a garden?

- Do you own the property or rent it?

- How much does it cost you?

- Do you have a mortgage?

- How much deposit did you pay?

- What are your monthly bills?

- What car do you drive?

- Do you drive to work or take public transport?

- Do you travel with work?

- Do you travel overseas?

- Do you have a partner?

- Describe them

- Do you have children?

- What are your friends like?

- How do you socialise?

- What do they do at work?

- Where do you go on holidays?

- Where do you work?

- Is it an office or outside?

- Where is the office?

- How big is it?

- What's your desk like?

- What do you actually do?

- What time do you get in and leave?

- What are your colleagues like?

- What's your boss like or are you the boss?

- What exams have you taken and what grades did you get?

- How fit and healthy are you?

- What sort of food do you eat?

- What exercise do you do?

- What do you give back to society, ie how do you contribute and make the world a better place?

- What are you grateful for?

- Who do you love?

All of the responses contribute to the vision of what they want to achieve. They have fun creating this vision because nothing is set in stone, they can write things down, laugh about them, erase them and correct them. They can add pictures of the things they want. Ultimately though, they have created their own vision, no one can argue with them about it, nothing is right or wrong. It is theirs and it then becomes relatively simple to use that to compel them to learn.

I would suggest that were this to be done at school, the next step would be to discuss that vision with them in detail to reach agreement as to what it is that they can achieve at school that will lead them closer to this wonderful vision. Generally speaking, this will involve them achieving certain qualifications and grades to achieve the job they want, and once they realise that, we are halfway there with the engagement. Sometimes of course it won't – for example if they want to become a famous musician. However, even that can be translated into skills and qualifications they can achieve at school. The same applies if they want to be a plumber for example. Plumbers cannot sustain a six figure annual salary without a good grasp of maths, English, customer service and even sales. Every career goal can be connected with what is being learned at school.

An important point to get across during this exercise is also for them to understand what a short period of their life they are at school for, what a pivotal stepping stone it is, and that at least 50% of the next 10 years will be at school. Therefore they are encouraged not to waste that first 50%, thinking that only the next 50%, once they have left school, will count towards their vision. We often hear youngsters saying they 'hated school' and it is such a shame that we have to then cram so much into such a shorter time frame to get them up to speed. If they are engaged to use this first 50% they will achieve their 10-year life plan. But vision is just one part of it.

Creating a positive mindset

Even with a clear vision, we don't achieve full engagement unless the young person really believes that it is achievable. There is so much negativity surrounding us all that it is very easy to be swallowed up by it and to believe that you are not good enough. We need to teach the young people that they absolutely are good enough, and that they certainly can achieve their goals if they keep a positive mindset and build resilience to deal with things that don't go to plan. We find that a lack of resilience and 'grit' is one of the biggest issues we need to work on with youngsters.

We teach them to expect things to go wrong and that when they do, to calmly consider the options and then select one to implement. We teach them to continue moving forwards – the 'you have to be in it to win it' concept – and to be certain in their own minds that they will never give up on achieving their vision. We teach the concept of 'power posing' and presence, imagining that they are handling difficult situations well and confidently. This does wonders for their real-life confidence.

The concept of moving towards a goal rather than running away from failure is also something we discuss with them. Both can be useful, however the former is more positive and more exciting and therefore an easier mindset to adopt.

A can-do attitude is something we emphasise. We all know colleagues who have this, they are life's boosters because it's nice and it's helpful to have them around. Compare this to a can't-do attitude. Again we all know people who have this and they tend to be 'drainers' who don't make you feel good. We encourage the young people we work with to be 'boosters' because it will make them nicer to be around, which will encourage their colleagues and management to like them, and in turn it will help them get things done. Hence there are several benefits of a can-do attitude.

We teach the idea that there need not be demarcation between work and play. The idea that 'I will finish school or work and then I can enjoy myself' is a thought path that we discourage. If they can learn to enjoy the process of achievement then everything merges into one and they can enjoy the whole of their life. What a shame it would be to only enjoy the times where we are not working, bearing in mind how much of every day most of us work!

Aligning life planning to business planning

This isn't just about life plans either; this process of setting long-term and short-terms goals is exactly what happens in business strategy and so has an additional learning benefit for the young person. In big stock exchange listed businesses in particular, long-term strategic business goals are translated into annual goals and monthly goals and then tracked. This is proven to be the best way of getting things done, and so if it is good enough for big business, it is certainly good enough for us to implement with our young students.

All these processes can be built into the curriculum with little or no impact on classroom timetables, and a goals template is included in Part 2 of this book to facilitate that.

Making it fun but serious – the charter

Obviously this process is a very personal one for each individual and has potential to go wrong if mishandled. Hence it is important to put in place a charter of confidentiality before embarking on this process. We discuss at length with our groups what is helpful to each other in this process and what is not. We talk about making a commitment to each other that we will respect each other's goals and dreams and be supportive to help the achievement of them. We promise that we will not denigrate someone's goals or be drainers to them and make them feel they can't achieve things. We make promises to do everything we can to boost them and encourage them to achieve. The rule of confidentiality is held extremely importantly, and from all this discussion we create a charter that we all sign and put on the wall by the door as a daily reminder.

We also set up buddy groups of four early on in our groups so that there is even closer personal support and so that support groups are formed early on.

Once this charter is in place as well as the buddy groups, people do feel more comfortable to discuss their goals without embarrassment or fear, and gradually, with group discussions and one-to-ones, the real vision can be drawn out and they really enjoy creating it and sharing it with each other.

Culture change

Teachers and parents may wonder why a school is focusing so much on life plans rather than delving straight into learning. For this reason it is very useful to carry out this exercise with the teachers themselves first so that they create their own vision boards. I have done this with my own staff to great effect. In this way they will see the power of visualisation and be able to align their own goals with those of the young people they are supporting. By having engaged students, their class will perform better and there should be less absence. This will make the teaching experience more rewarding and will also be more conducive to delivering outstanding teaching and learning, which will no doubt be aligned to the teacher's own goals in their own life plan.

If parents/carers are engaged this will also help the young people create their vision, particularly when they are at a very young age in years 7-9 and probably haven't considered this before. Getting parent/carer buy-in to this concept early on via some parent/

carer meetings at the start of school, and some communication, eg newsletters regarding why this is important, is critical in helping the young person stay committed to their life plan. Having said that, it is never too late to engage with the parent/carer over this subject and it can just as well be introduced for year 11. The whole concept will benefit the parent/carer too for their own life, which is a great side benefit of this approach.

Governors should understand the life planning concept and understand why it is being embedded into the curriculum and what impact it is likely to have on the outcomes for students, and be able to explain this to Ofsted. This can all contribute to more effective leadership and management.

A schedule of speakers to the school will also assist in this culture change. Rather than the school operating in a silo, the school can widen the understanding of its students of the opportunities around them by bringing in a range of speakers to talk about their career paths and lives. Local employers are always keen to do this and I discuss employer engagement in Chapter 8. Other speakers can be motivational speakers who are often keen to practise their speeches and so will jump at the chance of an assembly speaking slot. School alumni who have gone on to build careers and other young people who have gone through this process are always very inspiring to young people. Parents/carers often have great stories to impart about their own education and career and can deliver talks, as will governors. Teachers should also be encouraged to share their own stories of how they got to where they are now and the hurdles they had to overcome.

All of this will encourage a culture of sharing life visions and goals and working together as a team so that everyone can achieve their own and support others in the achievement of theirs. Once this culture can be achieved within the school then a huge step forward has been taken, and the next step is the roadmap of how to achieve the vision.

Tools

We have seen that a physical **vision board** is the single best illustration of their vision once they have created it; however, there are also other tools and techniques we use to reinforce the vision once it's been created. Firstly we encourage them to **present the vision** to their peers in class. This has a number of benefits. It builds their presentation skills of course, but what it also does is put a marker down in front of everyone as to what the individual is aiming to achieve. From then on they will have a **label** and a **niche** which their peers and probably even their friends and family will hold them accountable to. This is very useful to them on days when they are flagging or drifting. We have bullseyes in our classrooms depicting the targets within particular career niches, and we get them to select their niche and document it on the wall for all to see and refer to.

Next we get them to write a **life plan** for themselves and put it into an envelope addressed to themselves to open at the end of our course. The life plan template, which can be seen on www.1stjobseries.com, has space for them to document all their milestones and goals, big and small, and we find just writing this down gives them tremendous motivation. They are also encouraged to produce another one to keep in an envelope to read in a year's time. I have had the honour of opening these with some of the young people we have employed over the last couple of years and it's amazing how much they have achieved because of this mindset that's been instilled. Schools could use this technique to have a **new envelope** for the end of every term, and issue it with the school report. Key milestones for each term can include learning certain subjects, taking certain exams, achieving grades at a certain level, achieving 100% attendance etc, so it is all very relevant to school. The critical point is that it is relevant to their life plan too, and this is what makes it work.

We also use **small cards** for them to write their most immediate milestones on to keep in their wallet. These will be goals for the end of the year, the end of each month and the end of each week. We get them to write just the most immediate goals on to the card and to then fold it up and keep it with them always. They are encouraged to take this out and read it a couple of times a day, maybe on the bus, or before they go to sleep. This is personal reinforcement for them.

'Ceremonial ticks' is something we use with the cards – it is such a great feeling to be able to tick off an achievement, and this is what we like to do with them as they progress through our course. We then encourage them to continue this after they leave and throughout their life. There is evidence that ticking off goals actually creates a rush of endorphins in the brain that makes us feel good and happy!

www.1stjobseries.com has a template for life plans.

In addition we can encourage the use of apps such as Wunderlist, which we all use in our business and which is amazing if used in conjunction with Outlook so that items are listed not only as goals but also become real by being scheduled.

Success Story 1

"The system failed me when I was in school and college. While at school, with my dyslexia, I struggled with chosen tasks/work. I did not receive as much support as I needed. This was throughout my school years and as a result of this I really did struggle. Secondly, while at college, they failed my needs, as for maths class it was three hours long and for me this is not good where I cannot focus anymore after an hour. As a result of this I was behind and struggled, and they did nothing about it to help me. School was bearable and okay to deal with as I had my friends with me, but when at college, I struggled to socialise and talk to other people. This isolated me

from the group and I lost my confidence which led to me feeling really low as a person. For many months I was not in a good place and always feeling very negative. I was not the person I knew I could be.

"Since coming to MiddletonMurray, my confidence has been so high and I feel like the person I used to be, and this makes me so happy. I have socialised with a wonderful group of people and I have loved every day since day 1. The programme for me has been so fun, but also very educational. I have had so much progress and have had great support from my tutor and my fellow peers. It has changed my outlook on life as now I feel so much more positive and feel like I can achieve anything from what I have chosen to do. I have seen a difference since coming to MiddletonMurray as before I started I was really unhappy and really negative, but since starting, my confidence has improved, always smiling and being happy, and now I am a really positive person and I am looking forward to my future."

Student

From her parent

"Over the last six weeks my husband and I are absolutely amazed at how our daughter has changed. Her confidence has grown and we thank MiddletonMurray and their staff for this. From September to December 2017 life was very difficult for xx, and as parents this was very heartbreaking to see. We had daily tears and xx became very low. We made the move for xx to leave college and begin this traineeship with MiddletonMurray in January 2018. To see xx get up every day with a smile on her face, looking forward to the day ahead and come home of an evening and tell us, so enthusiastically, about her day is wonderful. We now just hope that she can find an amazing apprenticeship that will make her happy in her life. Thank you."

Chapter 3

Overcoming Lack Of Self Belief: Help Students Build A Step By Step Roadmap To Achieve Their Vision

Having a vision is one thing, but without a plan to get there it is only a dream and one can quickly become disillusioned with it. As soon as we have established a life vision with the young people, our next step is to maintain the momentum by helping them create a plan that can make their vision a reality. The plan needs to be all-encompassing and incorporate every activity they are carrying out on their course. It is pointless to have a roadmap that is separate from the 'day job'. Everything in the day job must be leading towards the vision, and if we are able to demonstrate how the school curriculum and qualifications fit into that roadmap then we can compel the young people to want to learn, and thus we have an engaged captive audience rather than a disengaged one.

The benefits of this are evident immediately: we see very little absence, a willingness by them to push out of their comfort zone, and a maturity that eradicates the need for discipline. I recognise that in schools these are issues that can significantly reduce achievement and that can be very distracting for teachers, so implementing some of the techniques that we have seen work will be of huge benefit to students, teachers and schools. A template for the roadmap is on our website www.1stjobseries.com, but even more important than the template is the implementation of some key principles which are laid out in this chapter.

Progression

A key component of the roadmap is the celebration of progress and the fact that every little item of progress counts towards the bigger goal. It is so important to build into their roadmap that they acknowledge and celebrate their progress. I realise that an integral part of good teaching and learning is to get playback from students regarding what they have learned, but I am including here the celebration of achieving all types of progress that will contribute to the achievement of their vision. There are a number of types of milestone, and if we can incorporate all of these within the school's life plan, we can achieve full engagement rather than only partial if they are also working on other aspects which currently they may believe are outside of school. We aim to incorporate all types of milestone within our programme so that the whole of their life becomes incorporated and there is not a divide between work and play. These include:

- Knowledge (reading, visits, seminars, conferences, research)

- Qualifications (coursework, homework, revision sessions, mock exams, final exams)

- Communication (written, verbal, email)

- Confidence (presentation, debating)

- Physical appearance (grooming, fitness, health)

- Relationships (friends, family, colleagues)

- Enjoyment, happiness, fun, relaxation (are they taking enough time but not too much to simply enjoy life?)

We encourage the definition of progress for all these aspects of their life and then get them to mark out progress milestones within each that they can celebrate. We then use the cards and the 'ceremonial tick' sessions to fully acknowledge the progress that has been made. This is critical in retaining full engagement and building momentum.

Milestones

As we've said, there are many different types of milestone, but they all need to have in common short windows of time between them in order that no milestone appears unreachably in the distance. We have weekly milestones due to the short length of our classroom programme, and then once they are with employers we have weekly milestones for a period of a year (we call them interventions). The longest period of time between one milestone and another should be a week in our experience. This is long enough for some real progress to be made but a short enough time horizon for focus and momentum to be maintained. Obviously this also provides 52 opportunities to revise and adjust the approach if necessary in order to stay on course!

Overcoming hurdles

Achieving an ambitious vision and a series of milestones is not easy and there are always significant hurdles to overcome in order to make progress. Hence it is essential to manage expectations about this upfront.

We introduce the idea of hurdles right at the beginning of our implementations. We ask the youngsters to identify problems they may encounter that might prevent them reaching their milestones. Then we work with them to not only determine solutions that they might come up with to resolve these but also to consider and manage their emotional state if and when these issues arise. We encourage healthy doses of realism and get them to see situations as they really are, ie not worse than they are but not better than they are either.

Where someone isn't good at maths for example, we get them to acknowledge that this can be addressed and then we put actions into their roadmap to address this. If someone is not good at English we do the same, maybe building in the reading of certain books. We get them to see the impact if they ignore these hurdles and that instead they need to acknowledge them and then get around/ over/under those hurdles in a variety of ways. The important first step is to identify these hurdles and fully expect them, but without dwelling on the hurdle, just simply acknowledging it in order to move forwards. These hurdles may be learning difficulties, home issues, financial worries, lack of popularity, or just finding particular concepts and volume of work really difficult to manage because they are new. All of these things can be addressed and then managed.

I always tell my staff and students that I go into work every day fully expecting problems, and that my job is to solve problems – expected ones and unexpected ones. With that kind of expectation, I am never shocked when a problem arises, but sometimes I am very pleasantly surprised when one doesn't! We find that once we teach our young people to consider solutions to problems but also to manage their emotions when they encounter problems, they grow in confidence and start to tackle issues as they arise without drama and without feeling sorry for themselves.

This latter point may sound harsh but we find it very important. Many youngsters come to us with a victim mentality. They often believe that their failure to have achieved what they have wanted to so far is actually nothing to do with them at all but everything to do with those around them and their circumstances. Usually they blame their school, sometimes they blame a particular teacher or a particular student who bullied them, sometimes they blame a previous employer if they briefly had a job, and sometimes their family circumstances.

Whilst all of this might be true, the real truth is that it does not help them at all if we dwell on that with them and analyse it. Whilst we may agree that it has been unfortunate, we concentrate wholly on what they can achieve from now on. We have a firm saying that 'that was then, but this is now' and we encourage them to focus on what they can do now and in the future to achieve their goals and to leave the past behind them, whether it was good or bad, and indeed find things from their experience that helped them in some way, ie the concept that life has been happening for them rather than to them. We find this is extremely motivating and can be quite a lightbulb moment for many youngsters who believe that they haven't achieved their full potential to date.

All of this relates back to mindset, and we constantly encourage youngsters to focus on what they are moving towards – their vision – rather than what they are moving away from – maybe a fear of failure, or insignificance, or their past or present home circumstances.

Tenacity

One of the recurring milestone checks is to review what has been achieved but also what is in the future, does anything need to be added to the plan and what needs to be adjusted or removed. Generally speaking, a change of subject is the only thing that cannot be altered, but once again, we discuss this upfront well before it might happen and use it as an illustration of the importance of tenacity in life. As we all know, achieving things is difficult, nothing is easy, but it can be made easier if we are prepared to commit and utilise our tenacity, grit and determination to achieve what we want. By focusing on subject choices which require a commitment of two years, we get them to debate and thereby appreciate the importance of tenacity and finishing what they have started. This is a key life skill, and acquiring it early on helps them overcome hurdles and stick with it.

We also explain to them that sometimes things might seem worse than they are, but with some tenacity, issues can quickly turn around. We had a case recently whereby one of our students once placed in work experience texted our tutor to say that they hated the job they were in and wanted to leave. Our tutor reminded her about tenacity and resilience, and of all the reasons to stay. Two weeks later, our student was texting to say how glad she was that she had listened and that she now loved her job. This was simply a case of her being outside her comfort zone when really she was simply within a more challenging part of her roadmap. By sticking with it she made the progress that she wanted to and was delighted when she did.

Freedom to change and adapt

We teach on our programme that there is freedom to change and adapt the roadmap as we go along and that it is not set in stone. The critical thing is that clarity over the life vision remains. So long as the destination remains clear then the route ways to get there can change as there are several ways to accomplish goals. It is also important to let them know upfront that they *will* change their thoughts as they develop anyway and to fully expect this. It really doesn't matter if their route changes. I have a number of examples of this.

My son Stephen was not sure at school what job he wanted to do although he had a clear life vision. He chose humanity subjects because he was good at them. He achieved good A level grades and continued on that path, reading English Literature at university. It was only in the last year of university that he started to realise that he wanted to be in finance. He continued with his degree but, once complete, he investigated what would be needed in order to make the transition. Having established that, he went ahead and took the various financial examinations, and as a result secured related work experience placements which ultimately resulted in him getting a job in finance.

Changing the path towards a life vision really doesn't matter and we see youngsters on our programme come in believing they want to do one type of job and leaving wanting to do another. For this reason the milestones we build into the template actually include checkpoints for the youngster to ask themselves 'is my vision still clear?' and 'is this route map still the best way to achieve my goals?' alongside marking off progress. That doesn't mean that we encourage constant swapping and changing though, far from it.

Integration with stakeholders

Having a roadmap which incorporates so many aspects of the young person's life can appear quite radical, and for this reason the concept needs to have the buy-in from all school stakeholders, just as the vision does. It is important to identify who these stakeholders are upfront and get them to understand and participate in the roadmaps. In this way everyone is on the same page, understands what the young person is trying to achieve and can support them accordingly.

Teachers

Teachers of all subjects are a key stakeholder. The roadmap must not be something managed by the careers or life skills teacher and separate from other disciplines. Yes it can be completed and managed within that function, but it needs to be part of the young person's school record and an integral part of the school review system, signed off by all teachers participating in the youngster's timetable and education. This will have significant benefits for the teacher as well as the young person including better classroom engagement, better behaviour and less need for discipline, thus better teaching and learning environments, thus better observation grades and better results, meaning that the teachers' jobs are more rewarding, fulfilling and successful. In short, by achieving this, not only will the young person's life goals be supported but so will the life goals of their teachers who each have their own personal career goals.

Parents

Parents/carers should also be fully involved, by discussions and newsletters. If we are to include non-educational aspects of the young person's life within the roadmap, the parent/carer will want to and need to understand why. I would go so far as to suggest that the end of term report is amended to contain a section on life plan and goals. Once again, the benefits for the parent/carer are evident in terms of a more engaged child, leading to less absence, improved behaviour, witnessing healthy drive and determination and maturity in their child, and ultimately the pride in seeing them achieve.

Funders and inspectorate

Ofsted, the Department of Education and HMI are obviously key stakeholders too, and in our experience, have been very interested and impressed to see the adoption of this approach and how its impact is reflected in their measures. For leadership and management, they have seen with our implementation a quite radical but robust effort to achieve the very best for all students, not just educationally. They have seen non-selective students who have 'failed' the system previously now fully compelled to learn. They see our approach as truly going above and beyond the common inspection framework requirements for an outstanding grading.

For teaching and learning, more engaged classrooms and more wide-reaching debates and stretched thinking and learning is witnessed when the life plan is discussed and worked on. They see how students are able to review their own progress and adjust their own plans so that they achieve the outcomes they want. For outcome for students, the exam grades and levels of progress do increase. Attendance and ultimate destinations also improve.

Leadership team and governors

Finally, the management team and governors of the school need to be fully engaged in the life plan approach if it is to work properly. It needs to be referred to constantly at governor meetings so students do not believe it is a separate activity managed as a sideline and separate from their school work. It is quite a lot of work upfront to achieve a point where every student has their own bespoke life vision and roadmap. It will probably take at least a week away from the beginning of each learning year and then another day from the beginning of each new term to allow the students right across the school to revisit their life plan and their roadmaps. This could be managed by having 'life plan' days at the beginning of term for every student managed by their form tutor.

Imagine if at the end of that day every student in the class had complete clarity on where they had progressed and had adjusted their next milestones accordingly. There would be renewed vigour and commitment across the board and it would give a tremendous injection of enthusiasm across the school. The management team within the school therefore have to see the value of this approach, fully understand it themselves by actually going through the process themselves, explain it to their own teams, and then monitor implementation of it through the timetable. I would like to see every governor and teacher fully bought into and involved in the life plan concept and then able to assist the students within their remit to create their own visions and roadmaps and then monitor progress.

By having buy-in from all these stakeholders, the school will now have a cohesive single mission for their school, which is that they exist to ensure every member of their school achieves their life vision.

Local authority and alumni manager

The final stakeholder is the local authority whose job it is to ensure that school leavers achieve sustained job outcomes. If the school alumni manager has a record of the life plan of each student, they are then able to personalise the destination monitoring of their alumni to a much greater extent. By being able to refer back to the plan when contacting a leaver, they are far more likely to achieve a response from that leaver and thus will be able to report fuller destination data. This will also be impressive for Ofsted too.

Another fabulous benefit of this is that it will also help the school to continue ongoing support of the leaver; just by drawing the leaver's attention back to their goals might help them continue to try to achieve them. The ultimate benefit of this is also that they will hopefully be willing to return to the school to speak about their career paths and maybe even offer work experience or employment to future leavers.

Success Story 2

Apprentice of the Month - Toni Ann Francis

Overcoming all the odds, perseverance through some tough times, dealing with shyness, constantly demonstrating professionalism and being calm under pressure were some of the personal and professional attributes that saw Toni Ann Francis, an office assistant at Barnet-based Bandana Ltd, being named as the winner of the MiddletonMurray Apprentice of the Month Award for November.

"Toni Ann's story is a compelling one which graphically highlights that with dedication, hard work and support you can achieve your goals."

MiddletonMurray

Summing up the judges' decision, MiddletonMurray said: *"Toni Ann's story is a compelling one which graphically highlights that with dedication, hard work and support you can achieve your goals. To be so highly regarded by her MD for the job she is doing despite dealing with, and overcoming, difficult personal circumstances is admirable and speaks volumes about her character."*

Toni Ann's assessor at MiddletonMurray who nominated her for the award said: *"Toni Ann has overcome all odds to achieve this qualification; she has persevered through tough times, she has dealt with shyness and now blossoms with confidence. She had a very bad experience in her first placement whilst she was dealing with personal circumstances and spent a lot of time with our safeguarding officer, but she never gave up on her qualification. Throughout my visits, Toni Ann has demonstrated her professionalism; she is always willing to learn, she supports her team and works extremely well under pressure. Most of her colleagues have commented that she has a calming influence in the office. I am delighted the judges have chosen her for this award."*

Speaking at the presentation of the award, Toni Ann said: *"When I started training with MiddletonMurray I didn't have much confidence, I was quite shy and didn't like interacting with people. With the help of MiddletonMurray I have come out of myself and I'm now fully able to interact with people and not feel inadequate. I have gained so much by doing this qualification and feel it will carry me a long way in the future."*

Angela Stone, Managing Director of Bandana Ltd, pictured here with Toni Ann said: *"Toni Ann is the first person people see when they visit our offices. She always greets people with a confident, warm smile. She is softly spoken, calm and always extremely polite and she carries out her duties very professionally. Toni Ann is a pleasure to have around and we hope she stays with us for a very long time."*

Chapter 4

Aligning The Student Life Plan With Parent/Carer Goals

I am aware and fully understand that some teachers are of the opinion that young people are their priority in schools, and that they do not have time to engage with parents/carers as well. Equally I am aware that many parents/carers do not wish to engage with schools, based on an unfounded belief that it's the school's job to educate their child and therefore they should just get on with it and there will only be communication if there is an issue.

My belief based on my own experiences as a parent/carer but also as a provider of careers advice for 16-18-year-olds is different. There is so much advantage to be gained if we can align the parent/carer with the life plan that we have helped their child create and turn them into an ally. This can most easily be accomplished if they are engaged early on and have a say in the life and career planning for their child. In my careers manifesto, I highlight the role of families as a key pillar in the development of a young person's career aspirations, outlining how the involvement of family can lead an individual towards more informed decisions and better resources. This chapter looks into this idea more closely, to explore the benefits for the young person's career aspirations of pursuing a stronger school/parent/carer relationship, forging a joint mission to launch the young person on to their career ladder and on their way to fulfilling their life plan.

Parent/carer requirements

As we are all aware, life can be difficult and full of issues, pressures and hurdles to overcome. Parents/carers face all sorts and sometimes helping their child with a life plan when they are so young can seem one step too much. Before we request their support and involvement it's therefore important we recognise those issues and make allowances for them. A list of very recognisable ones would include:

- Financial

- Lack of time

- Negative attitude

- Personal problems of their own

- Illness

- Competitiveness

- Difficult relationship with their child

Bearing these in mind, we have to step delicately into introducing them to the life plan concept, but if we do it in the right way they may see that it will actually get them what they want from the school and also support them to help avoid a repetition of these issues for their own children. For example, when we discuss with them the importance of creating a clear life plan with their child, and explain how this will help the child avoid some of the issues listed above, it could well strike a chord with them and they will be supportive because they want to avoid a repetition of those problems for their own children.

Equally they may actually consider the benefits of doing a life plan for themselves and this can really help turn their own issues around. For these reasons I think it is very useful to talk about adult problems and discuss how the life planning process at a young age can help some of these issues to be avoided, or at least equip the young person to be able to handle them effectively when they arrive.

Parent/carer issues

In order to identify the benefits of this alignment and engagement we need to understand the wants and issues of the parent/carer. Parents/carers send their children to a school for a number of different reasons, but mainly they have the following desired outcomes in common:

- Good exam results

- No issues

- Pride

- A happy child

- A good destination and career

- Help with behavioural issues

If we explore these we see they go a bit deeper, and we need to question this and identify early on the full extent of parent/carer expectations because these will be reiterated to the child throughout their schooling. Therefore it would be extremely useful to get a deeper understanding of these expectations at the outset. This way those expectations could be discussed and perhaps modified and aligned with the school's and the young person's, thus creating clarity for the life plan.

For example, the definition of good exam results will differ parent/carer to parent/carer. For some, only exceptional grades and specific subjects are acceptable, whilst others have a more open mind. The last thing we want is for a child to go home to talk excitedly about their life plan only for it to be shot down by the parent/carer. Much better that those expectations are discussed and agreed between all parties at the outset. If that occurs then we are in a position where the parent/carer is fully supportive of what the child and the school are aiming to achieve. If that is in place, when things go adrift, which they often do, we have full support from the parent/carer to help things get back on track.

With regard to pride, it's important for schools to understand what will make the parent/carer proud. Once again, this is related to expectations and it's important to know these early on. The same can be said for issues (ie what constitutes 'no issues'?), for a happy child (what makes their child happy?), and for a good destination (what's their definition of a good job for example?).

For these reasons plus the fact that many parents/carers do not have a network of professional friends able to assist their children, nor are they all as aspirational for their children as they have the right to be, bringing them into the career and life planning phase so early can prove not only very beneficial for the school but also for the whole family.

To this end I would advocate that a series of groups and one-to-one talks are carried out with the parent/carer at the outset of their child's schooling and repeated each term – to illicit the thoughts, feelings and beliefs about these and to get the thinking about how they can support their child to create and achieve a compelling life plan.

Parent/carer time restraints

The above does presuppose that the parent/carer is actually around to be engaged with the school over this idea of a life plan. Realistically though, not every parent/carer is or can be around even if they want to be.

Pressures of life can certainly mean that the parent/carer is not around for whatever reason and it is therefore much better to ascertain this early on and to also ensure that the life planning process is sufficiently robust that the parent/carer input is not strictly necessary. The other issue is that the parent/carer may not be able to allocate any time to this process but may want to be critical of the outputs. Again, expectations must be set both for the parent/carer and the child. This can be done not just via parent/carer meetings but via advertising and surveys and marketing so that the ethos of the school is understood.

It is also important, if the young person has had bad family experiences, to teach them the 'that was then but this is now' mentality. What has gone on previously does not need to impact their future. My son has a friend who was very young when his mother died. Throughout his important years of schooling his mother was very ill and his father worked full time. As a result he was often unaccompanied at school events and would come on family holidays with us. The school was well aware of the situation however, and gave him and his father an exceptional level of support. This resulted in him excelling in all areas and achieving great exam results, a great destination and a clear career plan despite the sad circumstances.

Another opportunity in this case is that the 'benefits of adversity' can be taught to young people in this situation and to their more fortunate colleagues. There are many case studies that we have all heard about the highest achievers being those who faced lots of hardship in their youth, often including a lack of parental support. We can use these situations once we know about them to teach the young person the benefits of an independent and mature view of their future and the theory of 'what doesn't stop you, makes you stronger'.

The important point is that if the school is aware of these circumstances at the outset because they have asked the question at the beginning of the life planning process, they can adjust the school's level of support into the process accordingly so that the outcomes can still be achieved.

Parent/carer unique support

Of course the other benefit of involving parents/carers is the wealth of experience and connections they may be able to offer, not only to their own child but to others at the school as well. I mentioned that not all children have parents or family with professional networks who might encourage them regarding their career. It is therefore a major benefit to these if parents/family of those who do can come into the school and share the benefits of their advice, encouragement and knowledge. For example, they may be able to come in and deliver careers talks, perhaps they can invite groups of students into their place of work for a taster day, maybe they can offer work experience placements or even real jobs or apprenticeships.

I have found in my work that very often all a young person needs is a role model and an understanding of what is possible. I often use the sausage machine analogy that if they come in and do the same things that their role models have done, on a consistent basis, then they will obtain the same results. So bringing in parents and family members to discuss their career paths and present options for the children can be of tremendous value.

I remember at a young age myself, with no real role models to emulate, hearing from my next door neighbour about her career in an oil company. It was this that inspired me to apply for a first job with BP Oil which I got and which launched my own career. We must not underestimate the influence a real person telling their real-life career story can have on the life plans of young people. We have had the pleasure of seeing this inspire young people in my business time and time again, so I know it works.

The school and parent/carer charter

The outcome of these early engagements between school and parent/carer are critical, but unless they are revisited and repeated the impact will quickly be lost. These cannot be one-off engagements and to this end I would suggest they are documented in a parent or carer/school 'charter' and then referred to in every term report and at any interim appropriate points. This charter should spell out the part that each party is going to play in the young person's life plan and what the rules of engagement are. Everyone should understand what the life plan is aiming to achieve, and everyone should define their part within it and agree that they are going to play that part consistently in order to create and achieve the best life plan for the young person, and that it is no one person's responsibility.

If the above items have all been discussed then it is far more likely that the parent/carer will play an active role and so will the teaching staff, and this in turn will encourage the young person to fully participate. Where there can be no involvement from the parent/carer for whatever reason, this can also be documented and additional school involvement in the life plan can be decided upon at this early stage and documented and planned accordingly. In this way all expectations are set and this creates a robust platform to move the life planning process forward to its first draft.

Success Story 3

"I believe that the reason the system failed me was because of the way that I was taught. I am more of a hands-on person, I always have been, so when in secondary school the way the teachers were teaching me wasn't the way that I learned, and I think the fact that they treated us like children even though we were, was the problem. I felt like I was never trusted with anything, and honestly thought I wouldn't achieve anything in life because that's how the system made me feel.

"I've always been confident, but when it comes to believing in myself I've only recently just started to do that, because when I was in school I was sometimes told I wouldn't achieve anything because I found it hard to

concentrate because of the way I was being taught. I didn't understand, so I really thought that I wouldn't ever have a career.

"Since coming to MiddletonMurray I love everything about the programme, strictly for the fact I've had many different jobs before attending here, but I have learned so much about getting work ready. I really thought that I was work ready before, but it has proven me wrong and I believe now that I really am work ready. The people I have met on the traineeship have been amazing. My class are nothing but supportive of each other and the bond we have is great, especially with my tutor. I really believe her methods of teaching have been amazing and she is mostly the reason I feel more than ready to start my career. The whole experience was amazing and I wish that I never had to leave.

"I now look into my future with confidence and self-worth, I know now that I am capable of so many things if I just put my mind to it. I honestly believe that I have a great future ahead of me and I'm so excited.

"I have seen a great difference in myself. When I learned about healthy living I had to make a change, I now go to bed every night at 10pm, when before I would go to bed around 12.30 - 1.00. I don't eat how I used to with lots of rubbish food, and I wake up at a set time every day. I finally have a routine I'm comfortable with so I feel that I have benefited a lot from being at MiddletonMurray."

Student

Chapter 5

Aligning The Student Life Plan With School Leadership, Teacher And Governor Goals

What teachers want

Engaged and happy teachers in adequate numbers is key to the success of any school, and as in any organisation, a school has to deliver career satisfaction and progression to their team in order for that team to be retained. It is my view that teachers' goals can be aligned in a very powerful way to the life plans of their students and that this can deliver the career satisfaction and progression they need for themselves.

As with all professionals, teacher goals will be many and varied. These will include:

- Exam success for their students

- Levels of progress for their students

- Enjoyment of their role

- Support from their colleagues

- Strong leadership and management from their superiors

- Recognition from students and parents

- Making a difference

- Career success from themselves in the form of promotions and salary increases

In summary, we have a life plan for our own life whether consciously or not, and the degree to which we achieve our goals will dictate the degree of satisfaction we feel in our job. By aligning the student life plan to these goals we can achieve true teamwork within the classrooms in order to achieve a common goal between teacher and student.

Life plan for the school

As an introduction to the teacher planning process, it is useful to view the strategy of the school in the context of a life plan for the school. Once again, we would ask questions like: what is the ultimate vision for the school, what are the key milestones, what are the key activities and what are the timescales? Once these are clarified, teachers can see where they fit into the picture, and hopefully the management team will be able to align the individual goals within the big picture of the school.

What governors want

The board of governors have their own wants for the school too, and as such should be encouraged to join in with the life planning of the school. Broadly speaking, at the highest level, it is the board of governors who oversee the strategy creation and implementation at the school and so they have the biggest picture. They want things like:

- High applicant rate and full capacity

- Good outcomes for students

- Teacher retention

- Adequate funding

- Full compliance

- High quality

- Low disruption and high levels of safeguarding

For this reason they can be encouraged to input to the life plan of the school too. What precisely do they want to see happen in measurable terms and by when? By engaging governors of all types and levels in this way, we can create a board that is proactive and driving the school forward rather than a silent committee that is just going through the motions.

The direction of the school in terms of its life plan is absolutely critical as it will then help the senior team and the teaching staff to assess where their own are aligned. This will identify strong synergies but perhaps areas of conflict too, and it is very helpful to identify those clearly in order to eradicate them and move forward. For example, if the board has in mind a minimum percentage of university places or apprenticeships, it is very helpful to know this as it can then be matched up against the student plans to measure how well they are aligned. The same applies for example to subjects and courses offered. If the students' plans contain particular frameworks that are not included within the school plan then the lack of synergy needs to be resolved. By creating this school life plan top down and then feeding back bottom up, issues such as these will be identified early enough to be resolved without adverse impact.

Teacher life planning

Once the school plan is clarified, and in order to achieve this level of synergy, it is important first of all to involve teachers at all levels within the school into the life planning process for themselves. By involving them personally they will see the benefits of the approach and be more able to convey these to their students. As with the students, I would suggest that a full day is spent on this and that it is done in small groups and one-to-ones. The challenge is for individuals to be open about their ultimate dreams and wishes, and then by identifying what is really important to them and what they really want to achieve, and envisaging this in extreme detail, they can identify an ultimate goal with clarity. What we want for them is a plan of at least five years, and ideally ten, which identifies milestones at the end of each year. Once they have those clarified they can then start to plan the next year in some more detail, then each month in more detail still, and then finally some really measurable targets for the current term.

What generally happens in this process is that the planner starts out with life goals; however, a huge part of these are career goals, and so for the immediate year's goals there tends to be a lot of career focus. This is where we can align their goals with those of the students. If a teacher has their own goals for exam grades, attendance, discipline, teaching and learning grades, outcomes for students and so on, these can be clearly aligned to each student. For example, by spending time with a student on their life plan, the teacher will be see benefits for their own life plan.

Teachers are in high demand as we all know, and good ones are highly prized and need to be retained. This concept is unusual and radical and focuses on the teacher themselves and not just their outputs and outcomes. A school that can implement this strategy successfully will be very attractive to a future employee and it would certainly be something to advertise as an employee benefit.

Whilst it's quite evident what teachers do want, it is also very clear what they don't want. A high focus on behavioural management and discipline is not why most teachers enter the teaching profession, and this is reportedly the single biggest reason for them leaving the profession.

In some schools, the amount of time spent on discipline often exceeds teaching, and although the teachers may have captive audiences, they do not have engaged audiences and this can be extremely demotivating. Unlike in a private provider situation, it is a very difficult process to have a child excluded from school and so the teacher has an obligation to engage with those who just do not want to be there.

I have found that the life planning approach addresses this issue to a significant extent. By having the teacher clarify what they do want from their own life plan, and then by having clarity on what the students want from theirs, a win-win scenario can be created within the classroom and this then helps to dissipate the discipline issue over time. When teachers can relate to their students on a 'bigger picture' level it makes for a more productive relationship. When there is a common terms of reference and single goal, it is easier for both parties to assess the value of day to day activities in the context of that goal.

At my company that specialises in placing young people into their first job, the first thing our tutors work on with them is their life plans. This takes a couple of weeks of full-time classroom activity. Firstly, the students visualise their ultimate goals in extreme detail. This includes everything they can think of including visualising how they look, who they are with, how they sound, what they are doing, where they are doing it, who their friends are and so on. If they don't like what they visualise, they are at liberty to erase it and just re-visualise! Once they have a compelling vision, they create vision boards, and with the tutor's help and advice they identify career niches that they believe will fulfil their dreams and make their vision a reality.

By the end of this process both student and tutor know each other much better and there is a mutual respect. The student has clarity over what they are pursing, perhaps for the first time, and so is significantly more motivated. The teacher has clarity too and can see new potential within the student and is excited that they can help that person to make a real difference to their life. Now both parties have a common terms of reference and framework within which to operate. The student will now have full comprehension on why the teacher is maybe pushing them out of their comfort zone to achieve the things they need to. The teacher will feel justified to guide and encourage the student towards that goal with complete conviction that they are doing the right thing. This is a fantastic win-win scenario that we have often been able to create in our classrooms with really great outcomes.

Succession planning for the school

Regardless of how happy a teacher is within a school, they may still have reason to leave. It should be encouraged for them to share their time horizons and career plans in order that the school can be in a strong position regarding their own succession plan. By being open about this, the school will be able to plan well ahead and teachers who want to move on will not feel anxious about doing so. At the same time, new teachers in the school will be able to see openings for themselves at various points in their own career, which will encourage them to stay after building up their experience.

Retention in any organisation is a key indicator of the successful management of staff, and taking the time to deal with the teachers as individuals to go through their life plan, although unusual, can reap rewards as I have seen in my own organisation. Often the demands of the teaching role can become very overwhelming and it is easy to focus purely on students and forget that there is a need for good outcomes for teachers as well as good outcomes for students. Teachers are in short supply and schools need to be innovative to hold on to good ones. I believe that teacher life planning can help to address this.

Teaching and learning grades

Having said all this, obviously the Ofsted grading of a school is of paramount importance, and it is fair to say that unless the teaching and learning in a school is graded 'Good' the overall grade is unlikely to be graded as good.

By implementing the life planning, I have seen that this can impact the elements that Ofsted grade – in particular the teaching and learning grade through making the classroom a more productive environment to be, and seeing true collaboration between teacher and student to achieve desired outcomes. Teaching and learning will be seen to be more relevant and the students will be more engaged. All of these factors should help to enhance the Ofsted grade.

Success Story 4

"*A young lady called xx was referred to the programme and I was told she probably wouldn't make it through due to her severe low self-confidence. She walked into class and was literally shaking. She was breathless and looked like she was having a panic attack. The journey was an arduous one, it required additional one-to-one support! When she did her first presentation, it was so emotional for us as she was shaking like a leaf, holding on hard to the TV! In her third week xx was getting better, after constant support, and she told herself that she was not going to be shut in this dark abyss anymore. xx made it, she successfully went into childcare and is now training to be a teaching assistant in a school. I see her when she comes in, and what a transformation, she is so confident now!*

"*I had another young lady in my last cohort who was also quite severely lacking in confidence. I remember a month ago speaking to the tutor about whether she would make it. I worked with her on her confidence issues, the other young people did too, and xx was able to overcome and is actually starting a new job today at xx as a recruitment resourcer. The whole office could not believe the transformation.*

"*Low self-esteem and confidence is one of the biggest areas facing our young people today.*"

MiddletonMurray safeguarding officer

Chapter 6

Aligning The Student Life Plan With Ofsted And Funder Goals

Working with schools, I fully appreciate the degree to which they are driven by Ofsted or an alternative inspectorate. The data dashboard is how schools are often measured, as are the league tables for colleges and universities, so it stands to reason why many teachers will say that whilst they want to spend more time on careers support and advice, they quite simply do not have the time. If, however, we could find a way to support the inspectorate drivers whilst still supporting the student life plan then I believe we will have found a win-win solution. My own experience of Ofsted is that even if the data isn't as good as anyone would want, they are still willing to award good grades if they find innovation and processes and procedures in place to improve results and evidence that this is working. I would therefore suggest that we should give as much focus to this as to the data drivers.

Inspectorate criteria change frequently, however outcomes for students always features highly. Destinations are now monitored by Ofsted and they are getting increased focus, not just for a few months beyond the leaving date but for a year afterwards. Destinations to low entry level part-time college courses will not score as highly as a high-quality apprenticeship or a university place, and yet the application process for these can still take as long.

My view is that if we focus on the full stakeholder engagement then things like the student and parent/carer view material will be far more thorough and insightful than Ofsted usually see. To have evidence that parents/carers have been thoroughly consulted and are fully involved in their child's life and career plan, which has directly influenced their activity at school, is different and innovative. By demonstrating this to Ofsted, the school is able to demonstrate superior management.

If the school can find a way to link the life plan and career plan of their students to the inspectorate drivers, and were able to thereby put as much effort into the former as the latter, we would absolutely achieve greater levels of students leaving school to go straight into great careers, and we would vastly reduce the youth unemployment issue. There are a number of ways we can do this.

Focus on outcomes

This is now a key measure for all inspectorates. Being good at delivering qualifications is just not enough to be outstanding anymore. For example, the Ofsted Common Inspection Framework now includes much emphasis on destinations, and an outcome of a low-level college place will not score as highly as a good-quality apprenticeship or university place. Colleges are driven to fill up their quota and will unfortunately offer qualifications which are just not of value in the workplace, but might appear exciting, just to achieve this. Often these courses have no employer involvement at all and are not even full time. They also have low entry requirements.

This can be distracting and disillusioning for the young person. We see large numbers of youngsters taking their foot off the pedal with regard to their final exams because they have 'secured' a place at the local college to do a course which only needs grade Ds and with little relevance to the workplace. We see young people start these courses only to find that they are bored because there is not enough stimulation as the courses are part time. They then leave and find they cannot get a job and become NEET. What we need to do is work with them right from the beginning in terms of their career objectives so that they do not fall into this trap.

Alumni tracking

We will explore the methods and benefits of this in a later chapter, but it's good to note at this point that if we can achieve our students finding something which does meet their needs, we can easily monitor this by using social media. Working with them while they are still in school at age 16 to set up their professional LinkedIn account means the school can then track their career progress and stay in contact with them, and thereby build powerful destination stats.

Alignment

If we look at what the inspectorates want, we can see that this is very closely aligned to what employers want. If we can get students to understand these employer requirements, and they are focused on working for a particular type of employer, we can align the goals of the student with the goals of the inspectorate and the school. Students really don't care very much about inspectorate grades but they do care about their own outcomes, and if these can be aligned, we can find that the students are indirectly working just as hard to achieve a good Ofsted grade as the teachers are. Some examples are as follows.

Ofsted want to see good maths and English skills, employers also want these, and hence we need to build into the life plan the need to achieve these so that the student wants this just as badly. Once they have a clear vision of why they need these good outcomes, they will be compelled to achieve them.

Ofsted also want to see good attendance figures. Employers want to see these as it is a mandatory requirement for a job holder to turn up on time! Hence if we can build this into the life plan of the student, they will want to achieve an excellent attendance record just as badly as the school does.

Ofsted also want to see good levels of progress and a certain number of these. Employers want to see their staff climbing an often steep learning curve and will want to measure this at review points during the working year. It is therefore important that we educate students that this will be the case and they therefore need to be interested in monitoring their own levels of progress. If we are successful with this we can reach a situation where the student is inadvertently working just as hard to achieve several levels of progress as the school is – and they will even be monitoring this for themselves!

Teaching and learning

Ofsted want to see good teaching and learning, but an outstanding grade will only ever be awarded where the outcomes for students are outstanding. It stands to reason that if all parties – and in particular the student – are jointly focused on achieving specific outcomes for themselves, the outstanding outcomes will be more likely to be achieved.

This can be achieved by introducing the life planning from year 7. By getting the students to see this big picture at such an early stage at school and documenting their desired outcomes, the teaching and learning begins to support the destinations and outcomes very directly. My proposal would be as follows:

Year 7 – The concept of life planning is introduced and some visualisation sessions are taught, including much class discussion, and resulting in a documented life plan and vision board for each parent/carer. This would incorporate three main points: a career destination for age 25; a statement regarding the qualifications required to achieve this and the ages these will be achieved; and a statement regarding why this is important to the person. The school term report should have a new section in it that includes space for parent/carer and teacher comments too. At the end of each term this should be revisited and updated by the student and repeated in the report. This means that everyone is very clear on what the student wishes to achieve.

Years 8-9 – This needs to be repeated every term. Importantly it really does not matter if this is completely amended every term at this stage. It is important that the student feels the freedom to amend this and that no career destination is too big or too small. It is **their** choice and no one else's, but just by having to write it down, and by the parent/carer and teachers having some input, the choices will be more carefully considered.

Year 10 – The destination can now become more real by encouraging the student to finalise their choices on employment sector and to start to look at different employers within their chosen sector, and for teachers to consider the types of employers they can invite in to give talks on particular sectors. The aim ought to be to bring in at least one employer to give a talk on every employment sector and career destination mentioned. This can appear to be a tall order but is certainly possible. I would suggest that these can all be done in assembly time, and that a careers officer can be hired at this point to bring in the chosen types of employer. This would probably be no more than five days' effort at a cost of £1,000 because, broadly speaking, there are really no more than four general sectors of employer, namely: Care & Education, Infrastructure & Logistics, Retail & Leisure, and Professional Services. In this year the termly updates and reports would continue.

Years 11-13 – These are the years where taster days can be arranged for groups of students within the four employment sectors. Students can identify their chosen sector and a day trip to an employer in that sector can be arranged; employers will often host this for small groups of students. It is also appropriate at this stage to bring in employability experts who can not only teach the appropriate packaging skills (see my first book *How To Get Your First Job And Build The Career You Want*) but can also bring in employers to interview for real opportunities. Again, in this year the termly updates and reports would continue and would probably be less subject to change as the student is nearing the final destination.

Schools say they have little time for careers support; however, I would suggest that this programme need take up no more than one half day in year 7 and then only two hours per term thereafter. That is only seven hours in year 7 and six hours in years 8-10 followed by one day per term in years 11-13. I believe this is a tiny time investment for something that is going to have such a huge impact on the student outcomes and hence the ratings of the school, and would indeed create a step change in the quality of outcomes for students.

Parents and Ofsted

Parents/carers usually care about Ofsted grades when selecting a school, and after that do not worry about it or even think about it unless it goes down. My view is that we can engage parents/carers to work as hard as teachers to achieve a good grade by explaining the criteria to them and defining what achieves a good grading. Most importantly though, this needs to be linked to the student outcome as above. By explaining to a parent/carer how the Ofsted grades mirror employer requirements, and that the student will only succeed in employment if he or she fulfils these requirements, the parent/carer will start to understand how important they are and thereby be interested in supporting their child to fulfil these requirements. Requesting a parent/carer view of the school through surveys will enable the school to check parent/carer understanding and support, and demonstrate to Ofsted that this imperative stakeholder management is going on.

When they visit, Ofsted will want to see these activities, and it is therefore important to not only programme all this into the curriculum but to also have on call a number of employers who are willing to deliver one of the four sector talks at short notice and/ or to host taster days. It is also important to be able to demonstrate the regular timetabled activities on life planning, job readiness, milestone reviews, and most importantly celebrations.

Parent and governor support

Governors and parents/carers are obviously employers and employed, and are a rich source of employment information and opportunities that are rarely tapped into in my experience. The board of governors do hold responsibility for upholding high standards within the school, and of course are involved in Ofsted inspections. My view is that they can be used far more extensively than they are to improve the quality of teaching and learning and to improve student outcomes.

For example, I believe each school should select a community governor from each employment sector. They should also select a parent/carer governor from each employment sector. This would provide eight employment experts who should take on as part of their governor responsibilities at least one assembly talk about their sector and one employment taster day. This is not too onerous for any employed governor and would hugely benefit the students. There should be much firmer demands on governors to share their real-world employment expertise rather than just attend governor meetings.

School alumni support

Some of the schools I have worked with have really embraced this with huge success. Schools need support staff and we have now placed a number of apprentices in schools to carry out things like reception and office duties. These apprentices can set great examples to the students because they embody what can be achieved with focus and hard work. They are also great examples to parents/carers and also to teachers who can proudly see the results of their hard work. Ofsted will also view this extremely positively.

So to conclude, the Ofsted challenge does not need to negate the challenge of achieving great careers advice for students. In fact the two can be firmly aligned in so many ways as I have shown.

A school can go from a place where they feel unable to do some of the careers things they want to because of pressures on time caused by inspectorate drivers to a place where actually delivering the careers support delivers the highest quality of outcomes for the inspectorate, and a true win-win solution is achieved for all involved.

Success Story 5

Apprentice of the Month - Robin Newland

A professional attitude, a calm manner, a good work ethos and overcoming personal challenges were just some of the attributes that saw Robin Newland, formerly of Sidcup-based Architectural Decorators being named as the winner of the MiddletonMurray Apprentice of the Month Award.

The judges felt that Robin, who has had to overcome severe dyslexia, was thoroughly deserving of the award this month.

MiddletonMurray said: *"Robin has now completed his apprenticeship and has worked hard to achieve his qualification. He is also an excellent candidate for the Apprentice of the Month in view of the difficulties he has battled with and overcome. Robin has grown in confidence through the apprenticeship, and his verbal communication skills and handwriting have shown great improvement. He has never complained, has had a great attitude and has worked extremely hard. He is now engaging with our recruitment team for the next step in his career and potentially to progress to Level 3.*

Chapter 7

Aligning The Student Life Plan With The Curriculum And Exam Goals

Concept of product and packaging

We often hear from school leavers that they 'hated school' or felt that it was stopping them from doing what they wanted to in the workplace, and I often wonder how they have been allowed to miss the point so much. We always say back to them that it is irrelevant if they enjoyed school or felt entertained, the point of school was to help them achieve their life goals! We get some strange looks at this point, and often we see the penny drop a bit later once we have been through the life planning stage with them. I think if we can get young people to understand the relevance of school to their life goals from year 7 onwards then we will eliminate the 'I hate school' phrase and stop our young students from missing the point.

In the programme we run preparing young people to find their first job, we have a number of stages. Firstly, we work with them to create their life plan and goals. Once that's clear and they have the right mindset we then get them to view prospective employers as the 'buyers' or the 'audience' and to view themselves as the 'product' that is being bought. This concept really helps them understand that in order to be attractive to the employer they need to 'package' themselves up so that they are of maximum interest and attractiveness to those employers.

We then do a lot of work on the different aspects of that packaging, incorporating obvious things like their CV and online profiles on LinkedIn etc, together with some not so obvious things around grooming, body language and articulation. Where necessary we also work intensively with them on their maths and English, because having understood the above concepts they become far more compelled to learn than they ever were because they see maths and English for example as part of their packaging. They understand that employers want the full package and therefore they work hard to acquire all components of that package.

It is my view that if we could introduce these concepts in school from year 7 and onwards, we would have a much more engaged student base whose focus would be to acquire the qualifications they need because they see them as a means to an end rather than a distraction from that end.

This chapter will explain how I think this can be done effectively.

Planning the curriculum milestones

The curriculum milestones are usually pretty much set in stone and so they have to come first within the plan. Obviously those milestones are per subject and will include coursework, homework, revision, mock examinations and final examinations. All of this is what we would expect to see in a curriculum plan; however, I believe we should enhance this with some very strong and clear goals at the end of each item as a milestone. So for example we might see homework plotted but the milestone would be a grade for the homework; we might see mock exams but again the milestone would be represented in grades. This presents a very clear visualisation of what they are planning to achieve rather than just a representation of the activities they are going to undertake.

Overlaying the life plan milestones

The next step would be to overlay the life milestones within the plan, representing all aspects of the student's visualised goals. Hence there would be career milestones such as a work experience placement in their niche, creation of the CV, setting up their professional email address etc. Another one might be a health milestone including maybe exercise, and other physical goals. There may be another one relating to relationships, another relating to hobbies, another relating to finances and so on. All of these have equal weight in terms of helping them become the full package.

Cross-referencing academic and life goals

Bringing these two sets of goals together is the critical difference in this approach. By demonstrating how each curriculum item relates to each life goal, the student sees very strong evidence that learning and achieving in school is critical to their life success. For example, if a student has identified a particular type and value of house they want, we can link maths skills to that, not only in terms of the qualification but in terms of acquiring the skills to understand mortgages, mortgage rates, savings rates and deposits.

Another example is with English where we can link the job of their dreams that they have identified to the English language homework because it will enable them to create a good CV, to speak eloquently at interview, and to write good letters and emails to employers and colleagues. We can do the same with ICT where we can demonstrate for example that these skills are necessary for things like job search, for budgeting and managing household finances etc.

The matrix looks something along these lines and will be different for everyone:

	3 Bed House	Audi TT	Job as a Nurse	Holidays in America
Maths Grade C	✓ Understanding mortgage		∧ Minimum entry level requirement	
English Grade C	✓ Writing mortgage application		∧ Minimum entry level requirement Writing job application	
ICT Grade C		✓ Finding the best deal	∧ Completing mandatory online forms	✓ Booking online
Summer Holiday	✓ Reviewing the goal, further visualisation, restating goals	✓ Reviewing the goal, further visualisation, restating goals	∧ Reviewing the goal, further visualisation, restating goals	✓ Reviewing the goal, further visualisation, restating goals

Obviously this is just an example and the reality will be much more extensive and individual; however, once this is committed to paper the student has a great point of reference. This can also be referred to at the end of each term at the review period.

The concept of balance

I have found that school leavers (and most adults) put a very strong demarcation between school/work and 'life' almost as if the school or work time is some sort of purgatory to get through before they can run off to enjoy their real life. It always strikes me that this is quite sad because we spend so much time at school and work that it does in fact account for most of our life! Therefore I always advise to find a way to make school or work as enjoyable as other aspects of life so that everything merges into one enjoyable time.

I have seen that the best way to achieve this is to identify progress that you want to make personally and then link what you do at work to this goal. So for example if you are trying to buy a car and need a certain amount of money to achieve it, consider the day rate you are being paid and look forward to each day that you attend as being one step closer towards that goal. There are ways to link every work item to a personal goal and in so doing begin to really enjoy every work-related activity no matter how difficult it is.

By explaining this concept right from year 7 we can achieve a more motivated group of students who really want to achieve maths, English and ICT for example because they understand specifically what that will achieve for them personally, and not because they are doing it because they are told to by their parent/carer or teachers. I have seen groups of students come to us who say they hated school and within a few days, by applying these techniques, I see them diligently learning their maths and preparing for retakes of maths exams. This happens time and time again so I know this concept works. School needs to be contextualised as a springboard to their personal goals and not an interim nuisance before they start working on their goals.

Holidays

You will have noticed in the goals grid that I included holidays as a curriculum milestone. I really believe we should have a re-think about holidays and what they are for and encourage our students to do the same. Very often students see holidays as an opportunity to forget about work and 'have fun'. They haven't linked the 'having fun' to work. We speak to our students about the importance of thinking time and how enjoyable it can be during a holiday to reconsider goals, what you have achieved so far and to re-plan your goals and strategies for implementation when you are back. Holidays can be used so productively in this way and are therefore an integral part of the plan.

Timetabling and turning goals into accomplishments

Once the curriculum and the personal goals are established and linked, the important task of turning the goals into reality must be monitored closely. Obviously this goes without saying with regard to the school timetable, but I am suggesting that the school together with the student and the parent/carer monitor all the life goals in the same way too. This can be accomplished in a number of ways:

✓ A daily review of the goals matrix at the end of the day where the student spends 10 minutes reviewing what they have done for the day, noting which goals those activities relate to and what progress has been made towards those goals. This is a tremendously motivating thing to do.

✓ Mandatory attendance at a weekly after-school club where the previous week's progress can be documented and recognised and where goals for the following week can be set by the student themselves to work towards in all aspects of their life.

✓ Mandatory school holiday tasks which are not just academic but also relate to achievements in other aspects of the life plan.

At my company we use something called Wonderlist which is an app that can be downloaded and is a shared to-do list. This can be very goals orientated and the list can be shared with others and updated by all list members as they add or complete activities. Hence a form tutor could share a list with each of their students which includes all of the life goals of the student and between them they can monitor the progress of these.

To conclude, I have seen that by linking mandatory academic tasks with the achievement of life dreams, students can switch from very disengaged to highly motivated people with a thirst to learn. We are able to do this within just a few weeks with students who have left school disillusioned and so I absolutely know that if these techniques are adopted early on in school this can achieve a win-win solution.

Ongoing Success Story 6

MiddletonMurray safeguarding officer:

"In my safeguarding role I come across a lot of students with issues, usually anxiety/depression, and most attribute their situation as having stemmed from bullying at school, where the teachers/school did not act, there was lack of support from the teachers, poor teaching and so forth. It is quite evident that some young people have been treated unfavourably within the school setting.

"Student B lives in an affluent neighbourhood with wealthy parents, went to an independent school and is 19 years old. Student B has been excluded from many schools. Student B has been involved in criminal activity, gangs, selling drugs and violence. Student B has poor reading capability, poor grammar, no knowledge of what verbs or nouns are, did not do well in

maths. Student B struggled in these areas and was not helped in school. Our test results indicated dyslexia, which was not picked up when in school. Student B had challenging behaviour and came to us one morning at 7am having attempted to take their own life by jumping in front of a train. It was a cry for help, mixing with the wrong crowd due to frustration and making poor choices. Student B mentioned having to join the bad crowd. We liaised with the GP for support and signposted for counselling. In class we delivered additional support and covered functional skills as well.

"Student B's parents met with us fortnightly and we worked in collaboration to engage and motivate Student B. Student B still feels let down by the system and spoke continuously about the experience and the fact of struggling in school and they thought he/she was being disruptive and unruly, but it was a way to cover struggles with learning difficulties. Student B spoke of being put in isolation at school and was so angry, hated everyone and everything. Took to crime. Excluded many times and went to referral alternative schools. Arrested countless times, beaten up, knifed and eventually left school. Parents were pleased that Student B came to MM and saw the difference from the support. Through holistic support regarding life goals, Student B has since achieved Level 2 in maths and English. Student B is still bitter at the way he/she was treated in school by the teachers and establishment. Student B is looking for a career in recruitment. Student B has come a long way."

Chapter 8

The Employability Programme: Aligning The Student Life Plan With Employer Requirements And Engaging With Employers

---

What employers want

In order to fulfil our life goals the vast majority of us will need to earn money, and usually that will be by getting a job rather than starting a business, particularly for young school leavers. It therefore makes sense to try to embed within the student plan the achievement of things that employers want. In order to do that, a good place to start is to define employers and their characteristics for our students who in most cases have never met an employer before.

The characteristics of employers are obviously varied; however, in my experience there are some that are shared across all, no matter what sector they are in or what size of business they are. These include the following:

Overworked – The UK is growing and that means that companies are busy because they are growing! Generally speaking, we are all now busier than ever and employers are no different. They don't really have time for endless interviews and they won't interview reams of young people for an entry level position if they don't need to. They just want to see people with the full 'package' of attributes so that they can make a confident hiring decision and then invest in training someone who is going to be interested in learning and really add value to their business.

Underfinanced – Growing businesses rarely have all the finances they would like. Because they are growing they are investing in hiring more people, more training, maybe more equipment and premises, and maybe more consultancy and services. This means that they are often stressed because entrepreneurs are ever optimistic and trying new things, but it also means that they do not want to risk wasting or losing money. When they hire a young person they want to do so cost-effectively and without risk. Hence they will be drawn in equal measure to someone who is not demanding too high a wage for their abilities and to someone who has demonstrated that they are a quick student with the ability and commitment to implement their learning and add value. They will want to employ people who are focused on adding value to their business rather than those who are all out for themselves.

Underskilled – Business is very competitive and as a result there is regular innovation within most sectors. Job titles are being created all the time that never existed even a few years ago. This means that employers cannot afford to stand still and need to continue acquiring new skills within their business. They will therefore be interested in people coming into their business either with new skills already, or with a proven ability to learn new things. They will also be attracted to people who have proven to be good ideas people and to people who are innovative and able to come up with ways of getting things done better or quicker.

Fearful – Employers do not want to get their hiring wrong. In the UK we have quite rightly some very robust employee rights, and as such an employer will often dread hiring someone who turns out to be a negative influence on their colleagues or department. They do not want to hire someone who is going to constantly be off sick or someone who is negative or miserable. They want to hire people who will improve team culture and help make their office a happy place to be. Hence during interview the employer will often be asking questions to try to eliminate those fears so that they can hire in confidence. They do have referencing at their disposal too to help with this.

Disorganised – Employers, no matter how large, can become disorganised and it is a great surprise how small details and opportunities can be missed. They will want strong organisational skills in their employees and will look for individuals who can demonstrate that they are able to get lots done in a calm and controlled manner. Being able to show that you handle a multitude of goals personally will be very attractive to an employer. It is also something to be aware of from the perspective that this leaves considerable opportunity within most businesses to stand out and shine, and thereby quickly become indispensable within the business.

Ever changing – Because of the factors mentioned already, most businesses are changing rapidly, and change management within a business can be a very time-consuming activity. Very often long-established staff can be resistant to change and this makes it very difficult for business owners to be as innovative as they would like. They are therefore keen to hire individuals who embrace change and can prove that they are capable of thriving within an ever changing environment. Resistance to change is a common downfall of many candidates because employers do not want to be held back by individuals interested more in their own situation than that of the business.

Ambitious and target driven – Most businesses want to grow and improve. Generally speaking, they have competitors they want to beat, new client targets, sales targets, reduction in cost targets. These targets will be hard to achieve and hence the employer will want staff who share these same characteristics and who can demonstrate a track record of setting targets for themselves and then achieving them. They will also be keen on employing staff with a sales awareness, even when not in a sales role, as these types of people will pass on referrals to the sales teams. Also they will want people who are ambitious for themselves and who have great future potential so that they can grow with the business.

Customer focused – Nothing is more important to a business than its customer. Businesses that really do well are ones that focus on the customer and deliver what the customer wants. Hence the employer will be attracted to staff who have a customer focus, and in particular those who can demonstrate their awareness of customer service.

Community focused – More businesses are now aiming to give back to their community in some way – whether that is providing free services or carrying out corporate social responsibility activities to generate funds for the less privileged. They will want staff who have an awareness of the importance of this aspect of business.

There are a number of other characteristics, but awareness of these main ones will really help a student to shine at interview. If the student can be made aware of these as early on as year 7, they will have much more time to cultivate qualities and characteristics attractive to employers, and also to build examples and case studies to demonstrate these.

Identifying employer role models

I have a concept that employers are the future audience of our school leavers and the future buyers. They will be the ones deciding if they want to give the young person an opportunity, and they will only be compelled to do that if they see value. Employers are everywhere, but it is important for young people to find out what sorts of employers there are so that they can build an early picture of the ones they would like to apply to and impress. Sessions with them to teach them where employers are is therefore important. They should include some of the following:

An introduction to LinkedIn is one of the first important sources of employers. LinkedIn is used by millions of professionals in the UK and across the world. The majority of hiring staff will have their profile on LinkedIn and students will be amazed when you can show them how to log on and search on LinkedIn for any company in any sector and view the detailed profiles of senior people there. These people will usually have documented a detailed professional profile indicating where they were educated, what qualifications they have and all the jobs they have held. It is fascinating for a student to look up some of these people and read all about the twists and turns of their careers, and very inspiring.

A particularly motivating technique is to look up profiles where the person attended your school or college because this will demonstrate the sorts of careers that have resulted (it is also a great way for you to build your alumni, but that is explained in a further section). I would suggest this session is completed with the student compiling a list of 20 individuals that they admire and would like to emulate.

Once students have had a chance to identify some hiring staff on LinkedIn, they can be shown how to find these on Twitter where they can then see the sorts of things those hirers are talking about and interested in. It is also useful to look at who they are engaged with as this can lead the student to look at profiles of other similar managers. Again I would suggest ending this session with a review of the LinkedIn list and adding on to it another 10 people – which would give them a list of 30 role models.

Having established a set of role models, the students can then be encouraged to google these individuals. Googling them will bring up not only their profiles but probably details of press statements where they have been featured, maybe articles they have written, conferences they have attended and spoken at, people they have been photographed with and so on. All of this will enable the student to really understand what it has taken for those individuals to get to where they are. They will start to understand that success does not happen overnight and that a career is built step by step.

Identifying future job opportunities

We must also take into account how the jobs market is changing. The fourth pillar in my 'Limitless Campaign' manifesto extols the significance of tailoring careers advice to the 21st century. There is no point in training young people in skills that modern employers do not require, or encouraging them towards jobs which will not exist in ten years' time. It is never too early to start laying the foundations for finding good future job opportunities for students when they leave. Encouraging them to start looking at employers and getting them used to being interviewed very early on will mean that they are ready when the time comes. There are a number of things that can be done right from year 7.

Building relationships between schools and employers

Most schools will already have some local community relationships with organisations as suppliers or partners without ever considering them as future employers of their students. It is therefore a fairly easy next step to start conversations with these about possible involvement in building employability skills in students. The best way to do this is to identify all those companies that the school has paid for services in the past and to approach them for initial discussions about getting involved in a regular employability programme. Not only will they feel slightly obliged as a supplier to help, but generally speaking most companies love an opportunity to give back to their community, especially young people.

The same applies to parents who are working; they will all have knowledge about different aspects of the working world.

Ex-students who are now in work will be able to talk about starting up in their careers and what worked for them.

Teachers from other schools, local authorities and other parts of the school network will be able to talk about their own careers.

All these groups can be used for the following:

Industry sessions

Although there is a multitude of industry sectors, we generally categorise them all within one of four groups. If you consider all jobs, they generally fall into one of these:

- Care & Education (everything to do with looking after and developing people)

- Construction & Infrastructure (to do with buildings and travel and transportation)

- Leisure & Retail (to do with entertaining people)

- Professional Services (everything within office-based services)

By having a regular list of speakers for assembly from all the above groups, young students can start to build a picture of the types of opportunities available to them. They can then start formulating ideas and preferences about what they would be most suited to and would most prefer for their first step on their career. These talks can provide the students with real-life evidence of what they need to have in terms of qualifications, and what it is like on a day to day basis working within these sectors.

Employer taster days

Once the students have had a few of these talks over years 7 and 8, I would suggest that a programme of taster days is set up for year 9. Once again, the contacts who provided the talks can be requested to organise these days, which consist of allowing a teacher to bring a small group of half a dozen interested students into an employer's premises for a morning to experience what it is really like within that sector. Generally speaking, these days can consist of an introductory tour around the premises and then a talk from one of the managers about their working day. This might be followed by a short networking lunch where the students can informally meet a variety of people from the business over a sandwich, supervised by the teacher. On returning to school, the students would be set the task of writing a report on their findings and thoughts about that sector and to consider if it might form part of their life plan.

Work experience placements

The natural next step on is to request these employers to agree a number of work experience opportunities for year 10/11 students who have expressed an interest in their sector based on the assembly talks. Expecting schools to provide all careers advice and experience, as is the case now, results in narrow-minded experiences for students when the world of work is diverse and full of opportunities. Our 'Limitless Campaign' has challenged the government to pull the responsibility for careers advice and experience away from schools and push it towards employers. In my company we allow these to take place throughout the year, and most employers will be willing to facilitate a few days for a number of students. If these are planned well enough in advance, you might find that a single employer can facilitate quite a number of students consecutively over a holiday period for example.

It is best with these opportunities to agree as much structure with the employer as possible. At the very least a timetable at the beginning and a report from the student at the end, copied to the employer, should be expected. Once again, on returning, the students should be invited to consider if this sector is still something they would like to include in their own life plan. It is also important that the student updates their CV with this work experience placement, being sure to make clear what value they added and what they learned whilst there.

First refusal for jobs

Having built up these connections and relationships with employers, the school should not be shy in requesting details of the application process for the next year's school leavers, and even if they could put down names of very interested students for a guaranteed interview at a certain date. Employers are always looking for new young entrants because this is necessary for succession planning and longevity of the business. Therefore, even if they do not have a totally structured intake process, it will benefit students if the school has secured the details of the person who handles applications, when is the best date to apply, what sort of entry level jobs might be available, and to have lodged a list of interested students with that person or department. If this is done by the school across enough employers, opportunities will definitely arise for some students.

The hidden job market

This leads me on to the biggest source of jobs for new young entrants to employers – what I call 'the hidden job market'. In my business we place thousands of 16-24-year-olds, mainly school and college leavers, into jobs that have never been advertised and never existed until we approached the employers to ask them if they had considered taking on a young person.

Generally speaking, when first asked, employers will say that they believe 16-18-year-olds are too young. We challenge that thinking with various case studies and talk to them about how a new young entrant to the business can address all their wants and needs (see 'What employers want' above). We talk to them about their succession planning and question whether they have a blueprint for this within their business, and how they are going to guarantee the longevity of their business as their workforce ages. This is often enough to encourage them to come and meet some of the young people on our programme, and once they have the meeting they tend to be very impressed with the quality of the youngsters and therefore offer a work experience placement and/or an apprenticeship. By asking these questions to all their connected employers the school can secure a number of real jobs for the school leavers.

Studying job advertisements

Having said there are a lot of jobs not advertised, there are of course thousands of vacancies that are. It is therefore important to hold sessions with final year students at schools, colleges and universities to start examining how to find these vacancies and then how best to respond. Most students will be unfamiliar with job boards and other sources of vacancies, so the first task is to show them these and demonstrate how to set up watch dogs and other tools to find as many relevant vacancies as possible. It is a good idea to look at a few vacancies in detail as examples of what is being sought by employers and to show how to read between the lines. Another useful part of this session is to discuss what would be best to include in a CV and covering letter to be attractive to the advertiser and to maximise the chances of an interview.

It is also worthwhile starting to introduce the fact that interviews are hard to come by, and that more often than not the applicant will be rejected due to the competition for first jobs. All of this will manage the expectations of the students and compel them to want to know how to beat that competition. Where they see a requirement for skillsets that they do not possess, they can build these into their life plans so that they are better equipped to apply for these jobs in the future.

CV writing

Preparing a CV with students is a very important milestone for their life plan. I would suggest that the first version is completed in a session at the beginning of the school leaver year. The first draft will contain six simple sections as follows:

- Personal details

- Key achievements

- Education

- Work experience

- Hobbies

- References

It may well be at this stage that the student struggles to complete some of these sections properly. However, this should be positioned as a work in progress to be developed during the final year as thoughts develop and accomplishments are made.

30-second elevator pitch training

Before we put anyone in for interview we always have them perfect their 'elevator pitch', which is so named because if the student finds themselves in an elevator (lift) with an important employer and is asked what they do, they only have 30 seconds to say something and so it needs to be good! The elevator pitch therefore has to be a punch summary of what is in their CV, but crucially with a couple of lines saying what they can bring to a company and why that company should hire them. This session should include not only writing the pitch but also rehearsing it, filming it and refining it until it is something that the student can rattle off wherever they are in 30 seconds flat, leaving the listener impressed and wanting to know more about them!

Interview training

This is a great session as it provides the school with an opportunity to instil some really crucial life skills to a very engaged audience because that audience (the students!) want to know how to secure a job. Skillsets that can be built during this session include confidence, clarity of thought, ability to answer questions clearly, good communication, how to stay calm, and good body language. In my view it is never too early to start teaching these skills to students. Starting with role playing is always a gentle, low-pressure introduction at year 7 and the interviews can be very straightforward at this stage. It is only once assembly and sector taster days have taken place and a CV drafted that the interviews can start to become job focused.

Interview training is also a good preamble to writing a good CV. Although the students will have a life plan it is not necessary for them to have a CV at this stage, but if they do it is something very useful to refer to. My view is that the interview training will make them think more about their skills and experiences and what value they can add to an employer, and after that they can start to put a good CV together.

Mock interviews with employers

Once some of these sessions have been completed, some mock interviews with real-life employers, but at the school premises, will be very useful. This takes the students out of their comfort zone and gives them experience of delivering their pitches and interview techniques whilst a bit under pressure, which they would be if in a real-life interview situation. They may also be asked questions that they had never considered the answer to, which is a great benefit because they can consider what the answer would be and maybe include it within their pitch and/or CV.

Another major benefit is that if the employer is impressed they may well remember that student and consider giving them a real-life offer of a job once they leave school. The school can encourage this by writing back thanks after the sessions and requesting written feedback about the students. Employers will be willing to give up half days for this in return for nice letters of thanks and testimonials.

Enhancing the life plan

The end of these sessions should be marked by another review of the life plan. In particular it is important that the information the student has gathered about their role models should be considered. If the student has found things to emulate then this should be written into their life plan as qualities or accomplishments for them to achieve.

Finding job opportunities for your students

To me, the panacea for all final education establishments would be to have every leaver secure their first job before they leave. In my company we do this with our students, and every school and college can achieve this too. Once the programme outlined in this book has been followed, you will be left with the two critical components to make that happen:

- A focused and employment-ready student

- Relationships with a multitude of employers who have met some of the students, know the school and have an interest in seeing the students do well

This is the perfect time to make real opportunities happen by speaking to the employers and asking them if they would consider taking on a young person. The school can then facilitate placements of their students and hold the interviews on their premises.

Repeating and refining the employability programme

The critical thing though is to sustain these relationships with employers so that they do not become a one-off. If relationships are retained, the programme will become better and more effective every year, supported by more and more employers. In order to achieve this, effort needs to be put in as follows:

Staying connected with employers

The school can set up Facebook and LinkedIn pages for their employer alumni that encourage employers to join, and place case studies and new opportunities on there. These employers can be all those who have participated in the employability programme, and the alumni group can almost be positioned as an exclusive group. An administrator would be needed to ensure that all alumni students connect with this page too, which would generate both candidates for the employer as well as new job opportunities for the candidates.

Regular newsletters showing case studies from the schools employability programme should be eshotted to this group, and the mission would be to grow the group.

A specific area on the school's website should be dedicated to alumni employers and students where the case studies can be shown and also the new job opportunities displayed.

What schools can offer employers

Employers often require more space to hold meetings, training sessions and so on. Schools have considerable space which is under-utilised outside of school hours. Schools could offer facilities for free to employers in return for them making a commitment to regular participation in the employability programme.

Employers often have rush projects to do, some of which can be quite admin or labour intensive. Schools could offer the services of a group of students to help on a short project, using it as work experience for the student in return for participation.

Schools can offer CPD opportunities for employers by giving them assemblies to present and involving them in lesson planning.

To conclude, I believe that a complete end to end employability programme can be set up in schools with full involvement and input from local employers, culminating in real jobs for school leavers.

Success Story 7

Apprentice of the Month – Matthew Porter

At MiddletonMurray we've always known that employing apprentices makes sound business sense and is an excellent way of assisting companies to address skills gaps. This was graphically highlighted recently when Bexley-based Matthew Porter, a photography administrator at Nigel Barrett Photography, was unanimously chosen by the judges as MiddletonMurray's Apprentice of the Month for August.

Our Apprentice of the Month judges are well used to seeing outstanding nominations each month, but not many that feature apprentice-inspired innovations such as the expansion of the company's use of technology, including the introduction of drones for aerial photography, greater use of social media, and the launch of an innovative new business by the apprentice, and his employer specialising in photography for same-sex marriages!

Robert Spurrett, Matthew's assessor at MiddletonMurray, said: *"Matt's role is to work with the lead photographers at Nigel Barrett Photography to help develop photo albums for clients and customers. However, he has taken responsibility for putting together new ways of working and is in charge of the new drone system being used to create aerial photography."*

Robert continued: *"Together with his manager, Matt, who is undertaking an IT Level 2 Diploma, has opened up his own business with Nigel Barrett Photography to promote the company as a specialist photographer for same-sex marriages. He's already made a name for himself with a very successful photo-shoot and he is in the process of creating his own website and promotional material."*

Matthew was the standout choice for the judges this month, as MiddletonMurray explained: *"Matt's only been on the apprenticeship programme for four months but it is extremely impressive what he has achieved in such a short time. His innovative business ideas, his acceptance of responsibility and his general work ethic make it highly likely that he will soon be running the company! He's an outstanding choice as our Apprentice of the Month and definitely one to watch for the future."*

Finally, Robert added: *"I am extremely proud of Matt and what he has strived to achieve. It's rare to find this level of dedication and his quality of work is without question. Nigel Barrett is hugely proud of him, and having a young fresh approach to photography has opened up new avenues and choices for both the business and Matt."*

Chapter 9

Resourcing The Employability Programme: How To Get Maximum Benefit From Careers Advisors

The programme outlined in this book for schools is simple, straightforward and, most importantly, proven. Much of the implementation can be done alongside everyday school activities, managed by the senior team within the school. Clearly though, someone needs to run the whole programme and measure the impact of it. Most schools have careers advisor support, albeit it sometimes on a limited scale, but the running of this programme need not be a full-time job, and I believe if they follow this template they will achieve significantly improved outcomes for the students. I want to outline here how to achieve this.

Sourcing careers advisors

Usually they visit a school on a freelance basis. Typically they will only work with school leavers and generally there will only be one face to face interview. The government awards careers advice contracts to businesses from time to time to deliver their services. The school can then call off these services and supplement them if they wish with private providers and coaches.

Selection process for a careers advisor

Schools should recruit a careers advisor based on a proven track record and via a rigorous selection process in just the same way they would any other position. I would expect any careers advisor to be able to deliver both employability skills **and** placements into new jobs for the young person, ie an end to end service. You will find many careers advisors only want to do the student-facing activities and have no real experience in dealing with employers, so you need to make sure you select one who can offer both services. The sorts of areas to investigate are as follows:

Employer links

Any good careers officer should have a wide repertoire of these and easy relationships where they can ring up an employer to ask for advice, placement opportunities, speakers etc. You would want to see evidence of their network on things like LinkedIn as well as evidence of their track record of placements. I would ask how many students they have placed with how many employers in the last 12 months, and also how many speakers they can call on and on what subjects.

Industry knowledge

You would expect a careers advisor to be able to categorise all jobs across industries and to have a wide understanding of the various industry types and the career paths within them. As I have mentioned earlier, we categorise all jobs within four main categories. This really helps students select a niche, but one that is quite wide. Your advisor may have a different categorisation, but it is important that they do have some method and not just sporadic or random knowledge. I would also ask how many students they have placed within each industry sector to gain an idea of any industry bias they might have.

Knowledge of career options

A good careers advisor will also have a good understanding of the options available to students for each path. Very often there are numerous ways to achieve the target career path. For example, a student might decide they want to be an accountant in a large company. The options for them would include attending university followed by joining a graduate scheme in a large company such as PwC. Alternatively the student might want to just do A levels and then apply for a higher level apprenticeship scheme with that same company. The less academic student might want to leave school at 16 and join a small local accountancy practice and do a Level 2 generic apprenticeship, followed by a Level 3 in AAT, followed by a Level 4 and then apply to a larger firm. These are just some of the options available for just one career path, and hence it is important that the advisor can demonstrate their understanding of this concept and show case studies where they have supported different students via different paths to the ultimate same goal.

It is also important that the advisor has developed and delivered full careers and employability programmes previously and can demonstrate the effectiveness of these.

Ofsted and other ratings

Often the advisors would have been involved in previous Ofsted inspections and certainly internal inspections. It is important to see evidence of the gradings they have received.

Funding

Some advisors will work for companies that have their own ESFA funding (government funding for schools and colleges). If this is the case it is important to ensure that there are no double funding issues that will become evident too late. Therefore, check if they are planning to draw down any government funding to carry out the work, and ensure that commercial arrangements are put in place to avoid the double funding issue.

Motivation and innovation

It is very important to understand whether this is just a job for the careers advisor or a passion. I have seen very competent careers advisors where it is the former, but there is nothing better than finding one with absolute passion. They engage with the students better, are much more determined to make exactly the right placement, and are absolutely delighted for the student when they achieve their goals. I also look for innovation, ie are they able to really draw out from the young person their true career goals, and then are they able to agree an innovative way for the student to achieve that goal, even if maybe the odds are stacked against them academically? These are the sorts of qualities that are found in really good careers advisors.

Time available

Many schools have a careers advisor but only to work with the leavers and only part time. I would advocate that the cost of a full-time careers advisor will reap rewards in terms of outcomes for students, popularity of the school, intake numbers every year and Ofsted ratings. A good one can have such a radical impact on a school, as we have seen with our own programme.

Resources available

Careers advisors will use their own repertoire of resources, so do ask to see these. In my own company we use a range of thought-provoking presentations, films, role plays, questionnaires etc to achieve progress. Sometimes our students will also achieve a small BTEC qualification in employability to add to their CV. A good advisor will be able to confidently run you through their resources and schemes of work.

Location

Some advisors will be so keen for a full-time position that they will be prepared to travel quite some way to secure it. I would caution against this as you really want someone with local knowledge and relationships with local employers. Having someone on board from out of town will cause a disconnect with the teaching team and students, so it is best to be avoided.

Ability to influence

Ideally the full-time advisor should be working with teachers to facilitate the delivery of this advice across all years starting in year 7. If the concepts are embedded within the day to day curriculum, as I have suggested earlier, then the culture within the school will change to be focused on achieving the student life plans. This is not a one-person job and hence the careers advisor needs to have the strength of character to outline the programme to the senior team and then coach and support teachers in its delivery. The careers advisor will of course also work directly with students in groups and one-to-one, but I would suggest this is best focused on students in years 10 upwards once the more formal employability sessions and engagement with employers is introduced.

Funding and cost

A full-time careers advisor will cost the school at the time of writing between £25k and £35k per annum depending on location. This is the equivalent to the revenue of between four and nine full-time pupils, or a similar investment to one full-time quite junior teacher. The benefits in terms of outcomes, culture, student/teacher/parent engagement and general student focus will significantly outweigh this cost.

How to manage the advisor

This role should be recognised as a senior position, and the advisor should be part of the senior team and also run their own committee. This will ensure that their work is taken seriously throughout the organisation and placed on a par with academic delivery.

As with all management, it is important to have clear agreement on the targeted outcomes, dates and measures upfront. Once this is agreed then the steps to achieve that also need to be agreed. There will be a number of sub projects to be implemented including:

- The designing of the programme

- Communications to all stakeholders (parents, teachers, students, governors, employers)

- Engagement of all stakeholders and methods

- The training of the teaching staff

- The planning of the timetable per cohort

- Timings and locations of delivery

Milestones must be agreed over quite short intervals and ideally the advisor should report back to the SMT and the governors at every formal meeting.

Growing your own

This role could suit an experienced teacher who has a natural rapport with external stakeholders and a particular interest in outcomes for students. In my business I have seen fantastic teachers make a really successful transition to employer engagement roles and vice versa. It is therefore a great alternative solution to finding an external candidate for the careers advisor role.

Examples of good practice

Success Story 8

Apprentices of the Month - Luke Ayling and Sarah Tucker

At MiddletonMurray we set high standards for our apprentices, and each month our assessors put forward talented candidates for our prestigious Apprentice of the Month Award. The standard is exceptionally high and so it takes something special to be selected as the winner. For our two most recent winners, possessing special qualities and being described respectively as a 'dream apprentice' and a 'great young ambassador' led to Sarah Tucker, an office administrator at the London Borough of Havering, and Luke Ayling, a business development trainee at Ashford-based Alpha Nano Solutions, being the standout choices as the MiddletonMurray Apprentice of the Month Award winners for April and May.

"Sarah, quite rightly, is described as being a 'role model' and a 'dream apprentice'. Luke is clearly conscientious and a very hard worker and is therefore a worthy winner."

MiddletonMurray judges

Sarah's assessor said: *"Sarah is the 'dream apprentice' as she has never missed a deadline, is always positive and is constantly pushing herself. She's always asking for additional tasks and has already finished 72% of her Customer Services Level 2 Apprenticeship, which is way above the progress expectations. "Sarah is a single mother who manages to balance her home life, work placement and college work around her two young children, Alfie age four and Freddie age two. Although, understandably, she finds it a real struggle at times, she has never given up. I'm absolutely delighted that her qualities and dedication were recognised by the judges; she fully deserves the award."*

Speaking about Luke's success in winning the award for May, his assessor said: *"Luke is 18 years old with no previous work experience, yet he has excelled during the time he has been at Alpha Nano Solutions, first with his six-week traineeship then on securing a full-time position as an apprentice with the company."*

Irene continued: *"Luke is the youngest member of the company, yet he meets with clients and arranges meetings competently whilst representing his company with professionalism. Luke is a great young ambassador for the Alpha Nano Solutions brand, both internally and externally, and I'm thrilled for him that he has won this award."*

The judges felt that Sarah in April and Luke in May fully deserved the accolades, explaining:

"Sarah, quite rightly, is described as being a 'role model' and a 'dream apprentice', which, when you consider that she's a single parent of two young children, who had no work experience or qualifications and who understandably suffered from a lack of confidence, makes her success at Havering Council even more impressive."

Speaking about Luke, the judges said: *"As judges we like to see people who go the extra mile get rewarded. Luke is clearly conscientious and a very hard worker and is therefore a worthy winner."*

Chapter 10

Maintaining An Active Alumni To Achieve Repeat Placements And Obtain Case Studies

---

Every school has a wealth of job opportunities for their leaving students if they are prepared to tap into their various alumni. Alumni are not just ex-students, they are various groups connected with the school that will not only have the ability to provide opportunities on an ongoing basis, but who also have positive thoughts towards the school and therefore will want to help. We will examine each of these alumni in this chapter and then suggest how to get the best from them.

Ex-students

Students who have left and are now working their way up the career ladder can be fantastic role models for existing students and they will often be keen to return to the school to give talks. We all know how fascinating it can be to return to our old schools where we used to spend every day, and often, students do not need a lot of persuading to do that. The important thing is to stay engaged with your students from the time they do leave, and the easiest way to do that is via social media and in particular LinkedIn. In this way, the school can monitor the career paths of all their ex-students and obtain some great case studies to show to existing students.

Ex-students are a great source of talks. They can come and tell their story regarding how their first interviews went, how they found their first job, how they then progressed within that role, how they moved up the ladder to further roles if applicable, and then most importantly their top five tips.

Ex-students are also a potential source of taster days, work experience and new job opportunities for existing students. At the very least they can provide the school with the contact details of the best person in their company to contact to see if these opportunities exist, and of course if they are doing a good job for that employer then the employer will look kindly on applications from students with similar education histories.

Ex-parents

Existing and ex-parents are a very important alumni group, and connecting with parents on LinkedIn as soon as their children start in year 7 is a very good method of building a picture of which parents might be useful in terms of future job opportunities for school leavers. Existing parents will generally want to maintain good relationships with the school and support them, and often if they are asked about where they work and who the best recruitment contacts are there, they will be happy to provide details. Ex-parents will also be receptive for engagement, particularly if their children do well in their careers. The school can capitalise on the goodwill this creates by asking those parents for details of their employment and who the recruitment contacts are. These parent groups are also a rich source of potential careers speakers to tap into.

Ex-teachers

A large employer group is of course Education, and there are lots of opportunities for careers within education establishments that are not teaching. It is therefore wise to not only let teachers talk to students about their own career paths but also to continue to engage with teachers who have moved on to other schools and different jobs as they will also be a great source of speakers and potential job opportunities in their new places of work.

Ex-governors

Governors, particularly community governors, will often have good professional networks and obviously a vested interest in great outcomes for students. These people are generally happy to introduce the school to their networks and pass on job opportunities and speaker opportunities. Governors are able to deliver so much more value than just sitting at governor meetings, and it is up to the school to get the most from them while they are in post but then to engage with them on LinkedIn to maintain an ongoing relationship.

Inspectorates and other authorities

These individuals should be regarded as allies. Yes they will often be inspecting the school and identifying where there is room for improvement; however, they will also witness all the efforts being made by the school to dramatically improve outcomes for students and therefore they will want to help where they can. Again, every one of them will be employed in some capacity or other and that will mean that they work for organisations that from time to time will have job opportunities. They will rarely be asked to provide information about the career opportunities at their own employer, but if you engage with them on this subject you will be amazed at how receptive these groups are and how much they can and want to help.

Past employers

Employers who have been into the school to provide talks are a very important group to stay engaged with, for obvious reasons. We see some employers who particularly like students from certain schools.

If a school can build that type of reputation with an employer, this provides a great pathway for a number of students in perpetuity.

Suppliers

Suppliers will be keen to retain the school's business and they will be aware of the competition they have to do so. With this group you can make it very clear that you would like all suppliers to provide at least a taster day and be a speaker for students once a year. This is not an overly onerous requirement for any employer, and with suppliers you are generally in a strong position to request them to do this for you and even to secure you one other referral as well.

Ways to stay engaged with alumni

Managing the exit process

At the end of a school year the whirlwind of activities can be very distracting, but the exit process is a crucial part of your alumni. Formalisation of this process and giving it due attention and time will give you the very best chance of keeping your alumni engaged. Ideally this should take the form of an exit meeting with each member of each group just prior to their departure and documented in a standard format. The purpose will be to find out their thoughts on their experience with the school, what they thought was good and what could be improved, and importantly how the school helped them and what good case studies they can report that the school could publish. They can then be asked to consider how they could help others in the same way via the alumni, and then asked to provide their details to become an active member of the alumni. By being asked in this way, you will have a more receptive group for your eshots.

Database marketing

The basic rules of marketing apply here. Firstly a database of all the names and contact details needs to be built. Nowadays things like MailChimp can be used to assemble a database of this nature, or a school may even wish to purchase a database package. This database is your main list and it is from this that you can run campaigns and communicate with the group to keep them updated and engaged.

Once you have the list you can continue to add to it and run regular eshot campaigns to provide case studies where the alumni has really helped start the career of one of your students. These case studies are the absolute best way to demonstrate the value they can easily add to help change a young person's future. The more of these the school has, the better. Systems like MailChimp will have an inbuilt unsubscribe button so there is no issue with regular eshotting, and the more often, the better.

Obviously the job of obtaining the contact details in the first place for all historic members is quite a big one. However, if this is done consistently it need not be a mammoth task once the historic members are collated. To start to build the historic ones I would suggest the following steps:

- Review records for the last five years of all parents, teachers, governors and students who have left in the past five years. Add their email addresses to the database if available, being sure to identify which group they belong to as you will want to send different emails to the different groups.

- Look them all up on LinkedIn and Facebook to supplement the information you already hold, in particular current employer and job title, and add to the database.

- Google them to also find supplementary information.

I estimate you will obtain at least 50% of the email addresses this way, probably more, and this is a very good place to start. I would then send an introductory email explaining that the school is building an alumni of important ex-friends of the school in order to secure potential job-related opportunities for existing parents and students. Once this is sent you will inevitably receive a few unsubscribes, a few 'bounce backs' where the email address no longer exists, and maybe even a few unpleasant or derogatory emails from people who maybe had a complaint in the past. All this is very normal and you will then be left with a clean database that you can work on.

For all new members, the collection of new parent, teacher, student, governor and other groups can be obtained much more easily. Have a mechanism in place whereby they are requested to provide email and job title details as part of their first contact with the school. You can then have an eshot programme with them for the duration of their relationship with the school which can then continue easily after they have left.

Awards events

The school can also use the list to invite the group to alumni events (don't forget there are potential networking benefits for the members too by meeting each other). The crucial point is that every single communication must have a 'call for action', ie a request for information relating to any taster day, work experience or job opportunities at their places of work or anywhere else they know.

To summarise, I suggest the school maintains a database group of contacts in each of the alumni groups and eshots them at least monthly with at least one case study where someone in the alumni has helped a student with job opportunities. This is then followed by a very clear call for action for someone else in the group to do the same. In this way you will enjoy a perpetual source of opportunities for your students to set them on their path.

Success Story 9

Apprentice of the Month - Claudia Alexandrescu

There are many factors that the judges take into consideration when choosing which of the shortlisted nominees is more deserving of our coveted Apprentice of the Month Award. These include the report from their assessor, their progress on the apprenticeship, and any testimonial statements from their employer.

However, such is the consistent high standard of the apprentices nominated that it's often the additional information supplied that makes all the difference for the judges. That was certainly the case when Hornchurch-based Claudia Alexandrescu, a junior accountant at C & C Taxation Services Limited, was unanimously chosen as the MiddletonMurray Apprentice of the Month for April.

Alongside the information on Claudia's excellent progress at work, and the update on her dedication to pass her AAT Level 3 exams, the judges also heard how Claudia undertook and passed her English Level 2 exams to help her to overcome the fact that English is not her first language. There was also the small matter that all this was being undertaken whilst also being the mother to two small children!

Claudia was nominated by her assessor, Emma Emanuel, who said: *"Claudia works four days a week at C & C Taxation Services and studies with MiddletonMurray on the other day. Claudia is incredibly dedicated to her studies and always attends class, remains behind to do extra studying and works late into the night at home."*

Emma added: *"To her great credit, it is incredibly important to Claudia that she sets the right example to her children by teaching them the correct work ethic and I'm delighted she's won this award."*

Claudia's employer Robert Copeland made this very honest statement in support of her nomination: *"When Claudia joined us in September 2016, she was told that she was 'very fortunate' that we offered her the apprenticeship. However, it's now clear that we were the fortunate ones to be able to secure her services."*

The judges said: *"The fact that Claudia is doing so well at the accountancy company is all the more impressive considering that English is not her first language. When you also consider that Claudia is a mother to two young children, yet maintains her strong focus on working hard and achieving success to set a good example to her children, there really was only one winner we could choose and we are delighted for her."*

PART 2
ACTIONABLE TOOLS AND TEMPLATES

The MiddletonMurray Traineeship Scheme of Works

A complete overview of our programme that has nurtured the aspirations and built the careers of thousands of young people over the past seven years. A blueprint to pick up and implement.

- Employability and Life Planning

- Personal Branding

- Social Media

- Customer Service

- You and the World of Work

- Project Work

- Five-year goals template

- Life plan template

- Life plan and career progression template

- Niche/sectors of work template

Employability and Life Planning

Traineeship					
Employability and Life Planning					
Lesson	Learning Objectives	Outline of Lesson	Keywords	What Students Produce	Success Criteria
Induction and Life Plan	Today students will recap Thursday's induction afternoon Complete IA diagnostics Recap expectations Health & Safety and Housekeeping E portfolio activation Life plan first draft	Discussing life plans Making a start on life plans including intrinsic and extrinsic motivations Completion of functional skills diagnostics	Life plan Work ready First aiders Evacuation procedures Niche Intrinsic motivation Extrinsic motivation	First draft of life plan based on life plan templates	Be able to identify first aiders Identify their motivation Identify their niche Complete first draft of life plan

Traineeship

Employability and Life Planning

Lesson	Learning Objectives	Outline of Lesson	Keywords	What Students Produce	Success Criteria
Job Search and 3 Sectors	Name 3 sectors Private/public/voluntary Understand the difference between sectors Identify where to look for jobs Complete a SWOT analysis Name 5 headings on a CV	To introduce students to the 3 sectors in order to identify what they might want to do as a career Learn how to write a professional looking CV, what should and shouldn't be included Screening CVs	Curriculum vitae SWOT analysis Public/private /voluntary sectors Personal profile	A presentation on a company in one of the 3 sectors A personal SWOT analysis	To be able to present a job role and company from the private, public or voluntary sector to their group Name the headings that should be used in a CV Screen CVs and explain reasons for accepting or rejecting them

Employability and Life Planning

Traineeship					
Employability and Life Planning					
Lesson	Learning Objectives	Outline of Lesson	Keywords	What Students Produce	Success Criteria
CV Writing and Covering Letters	Be able to write a professional CV	To identify the success criteria for a CV and write one	Covering letter	A CV	Completion of a grammatically correct, professional looking CV
	Be able to explain how to create a professional persona	Write a professional sounding covering letter and complete application forms	CV	A covering letter	Completion of a grammatically correct, covering letter
	Be able to write a professional sounding covering letter		Application forms	An application form	
	To introduce yourself with confidence				
	Be able to put together an application				

Traineeship

Employability and Life Planning

Lesson	Learning Objectives	Outline of Lesson	Keywords	What Students Produce	Success Criteria
Interview Preparation	List 5 important things to do in preparation for interview Identify and explain at least 3 ways to research a company effectively Understand the importance of journey planning	To introduce company research and understand why it is important Looking at making a professional impression prior to interview via email and understand the importance of planning	Company research Journey planning Job briefs Speaking and listening	A research booklet to refer to A detailed journey plan A professional email confirmation to an interview invitation	Be able to talk about their company from their research Have a good understanding of why planning is important Successfully confirm their attendance for an interview
Mock Interviews	To be able to present themselves for interview punctually To answer interview questions appropriately Evaluate their performance	To attend a mock interview with their tutor and present themselves in a positive way showing they have prepared	Skills Qualities What they can offer	An evaluation of their performance	To perform well enough to be offered a job

Life Planning – Personal Branding

Traineeship					
Life Planning – Personal Branding					
Lesson	Learning Objectives	Outline of Lesson	Keywords	What Students Produce	Success Criteria
Your Brand	To identify your archetype List appropriate attire for interviews for both men and women Identify 2 mannerisms and what impression they give List at least 2 USPs for yourself Identify 3 potential testimonials Be able to answer 5 interview Qs using STAR List 4 types of interviews	To introduce the concept of archetypes so we can identify with personality traits and how this can link into our chosen career To gain a better understanding of ourselves so we can market ourselves better Introduce the STAR method of answering interview questions effectively	STAR method Archetype Mannerisms USPs Testimonials	A PowerPoint presentation on how to be successful at different types of interviews Record a suitable voicemail and email address for when in the job market	Delivery of PowerPoint presentation and peer assessment of colleagues' work Identifying potential testimonials to collect for future projects Be able to introduce themselves confidently to their colleagues

Traineeship

Life Planning – Personal Branding

Lesson	Learning Objectives	Outline of Lesson	Keywords	What Students Produce	Success Criteria
Your Pitch	To create an elevator pitch to market yourself or to use in interviews To list 6 things you can do to ensure you are work ready Attend a group interview and evaluate your performance	To introduce the concept of elevator pitches and when to use them Understand what work readiness means and how to demonstrate this in the workplace Prepare for 2nd mock interview to apply new knowledge	Elevator pitch Work readiness Evaluation	A short elevator pitch to introduce/ sell themselves An evaluation of their performance in a group interview Research for 2nd mock interview including journey plan	Delivery of an elevator pitch recorded and delivered to time Complete and honest evaluation of their group interview performance together with feedback and what they need to work on
2nd Mock Interviews	To perform well in an interview: Arrive on time Delivery or incorporate elevator pitch	Conduct 1-2-1 interviews to allow trainees to apply new learning and demonstrate appropriate interview technique	USPs Testimonials Strengths/ weaknesses	They should have research prep from the previous day	To arrive on time and prepared for job interview Gain positive feedback from interviewer

Life Planning – Personal Branding

Traineeship					
Life Planning – Personal Branding					
Lesson	Learning Objectives	Outline of Lesson	Keywords	What Students Produce	Success Criteria
Self-Management	Identify 2 examples of how you can manage yourself To write an account of where you think you need to improve your self-management Prioritise your day List 5 key elements to staying healthy Create a healthy menu for a week together with the calorific/nutritional value	To understand how managing ourselves is important and what we need to do to ensure we are able to work independently and display the right attitudes and behaviours at work Understand how to stay healthy to be able to sustain employment	Self-management Prioritisation Junk sleep Hydration	A to do list prioritised correctly to make the most of their time and to ensure all tasks are completed A healthy living plan to help sustain fitness levels to be able to ensure good attendance and maintain energy levels for a working day	A completed to-do list appropriately prioritised A completed evaluation of their current level of self-management A comprehensive plan for staying healthy at work

Traineeship

Life Planning – Personal Branding

Lesson	Learning Objectives	Outline of Lesson	Keywords	What Students Produce	Success Criteria
Professionalism Your Brand Presentation	List 4 things to do on your first day at work to demonstrate professionalism	To gain an understanding of how to demonstrate professionalism at work To create a 5 minute personal presentation to market yourself to employers	Professionalism Probation	A 5 minute personal presentation	Delivery of a personal pitch encompassing elevator pitch USPs and testimonials to time

Employability – Social Media

Traineeship					
Employability – Social Media					
Lesson	Learning Objectives	Outline of Lesson	Keywords	What Students Produce	Success Criteria
Social Media – how safe is it?	List at least 4 social media platforms List 4 ways to stay safe online How social media can affect your job search Create your professional identity language appropriate for the workplace Describe active listening and how to demonstrate this	To explore safety online and how what you post can affect your job search both negatively and positively Introduce and explore a speculative approach to job hunting Identify barriers and how to overcome them	CEOP Networking Professional Social media Speculative Active listening	A professional LinkedIn profile A piece of research on how posting irresponsibly has had negative implications on peoples' lives	Trainees to take a fresh look at their social media presence and update accordingly A grammatically correct, professional looking LinkedIn profile

Traineeship

Employability – Social Media

Lesson	Learning Objectives	Outline of Lesson	Keywords	What Students Produce	Success Criteria
LinkedIn Profiles	Create a professional LinkedIn profile	Create a professional social media profile to show you in the best possible light	Media presence	A script to help them introduce themselves on spec	A grammatically correct, professional looking LinkedIn profile
Promotional Video	Begin preparation for creating a promotional video	Look at using video editing technology to create a personal promotional video			The plan for the creation of a 5 minute or less promotional video encompassing testimonials and USPs
Video Editing	To finalise and complete their personal promotional video	To use video editing technology to complete their promotional video	WeVideo Editing	A promotional video of themselves	Completion and screening in class of their promotional video

Employability – Social Media

Traineeship				
Employability – Social Media				
Lesson	Learning Objectives	Outline of Lesson	Keywords	What Students Produce	Success Criteria
You and Your Finances	Identify the difference between needs and wants List what should be on a payslip Identify what you would raise taxes on and why List 3 pros and cons of a bank account Calculate the tax for different tax bands To create a set of costings for furnishing your first home Staying within budget	To introduce the concept of budgeting and managing your own money To introduce the difference between needs and wants Outline how taxation in the UK operates and what you can expect to pay To understand the concept of budgeting to live independently To gain an understanding of what things cost and how to afford these on a budget	Needs Wants Budgeting Taxation Banking Pay day loans Payslip Net pay Gross pay National Insurance Tax code Budget Value for money Income Outgoings Ongoing costs Expenses	A presentation on increasing a tax, why it should be increased and what you would spend it on Calculations on potential earnings A spreadsheet of costings for furnishing their first home on a budget	Delivering a presentation arguing a raise in tax and what it should be spent on Keeping costs down, getting value for money and staying within budget

Traineeship

Employability – Social Media

Lesson	Learning Objectives	Outline of Lesson	Keywords	What Students Produce	Success Criteria
Dragons' Den	To identify and pitch a product or service that peers want to invest in End of week report	To work in pairs to identify, plan and pitch a business idea to the 'Dragons'	Business proposal Pitch Objections Target audience	Create a business plan/model for their product or service Create a persuasive pitch to encourage 'Dragons' to invest Weekly progress report	To persuade at least 1 'Dragon' to invest in their product/service

Customer Service

Traineeship					
Customer Service					
Lesson	Learning Objectives	Outline of Lesson	Keywords	What Students Produce	Success Criteria
Internal and External Customers Equality and Diversity	List/identify 5 customer expectations List 8 protected characteristics Describe two ways you can support diversity in the workplace	To introduce the concept of internal and external customers and their expectations To gain an understanding of E & D and the current legislation	Expectations Internal customers External customers Protected characteristics Diversity	Research around equality legislation PowerPoint presentation on customer expectations and how this links to customer satisfaction	Be able to outline current equality legislation, describe protected characteristics and how diversity can be supported in the workplace

Traineeship

Customer Service

Lesson	Learning Objectives	Outline of Lesson	Keywords	What Students Produce	Success Criteria
Health & Safety	List 6 key points on an induction	Introduce the importance of Health & Safety in the workplace and how H & S is everyone's responsibility	Induction	Research on HASAWA	To discuss Health & Safety and how it links to the workplace
First Aid	Describe the difference between a hazard and a risk		HASAWA	H & S presentation	
Policies and Procedures	List 5 common causes of fire		Health & Safety	An infomercial about H & S	Creation of written work outlining H & S legislations
	State the 3 key aims of first aid	Raise fire safety awareness	Hazard and rise		Working collaboratively to create an infomercial
	List the contents of a first aid box	Outline basic first aid and who it relates to in the workplace	Signs and symbols		To list the contents of a first aid box and describe the needs and duties of an appointed person
	Explain the difference between a policy and a procedure		Primary and secondary survey		
			Appointed person		
			Accident reporting		

Customer Service

Traineeship				
Customer Service				
Lesson	Learning Objectives	Outline of Lesson	Keywords	What Students Produce	Success Criteria
Knowledge of Products and Services	Describe the difference between verbal and non-verbal communication	To introduce communication and customer service language and be able to change your approach to suit your audience	Trade organisations	8 short customer role play scripts to demonstrate knowledge – to be peer assessed	To successfully role play customer service scripts to demonstrate knowledge and correct use of customer service language
Communication in Customer Service	List 4 common sources of information for customers		Promotion		
			Verbal		
Role Plays	Write 8 short customer service role play scripts	Put into practice customer service knowledge and language by creating scripts	Non-verbal	Marketing material for role plays	
			Products and services		
			Reputation		
			Trust		

Traineeship

Customer Service

Lesson	Learning Objectives	Outline of Lesson	Keywords	What Students Produce	Success Criteria
Telephone Workshop	List 4 features of a business telephone Take an accurate and grammatically correct telephone message	To understand the importance of using the telephone in a business environment To introduce business ethics and why they are important	Ethics Excellence Whistleblowing Honesty Action plan Principles	An accurate and grammatically correct telephone message	To discuss ethics and principles and why these are important in business
Business Ethics and Whistleblowing	Explain what whistleblowing is	Gain an understanding of whistleblowing		Research on a whistleblowing case to discuss with colleagues	

Customer Service

Traineeship					
Customer Service					
Lesson	Learning Objectives	Outline of Lesson	Keywords	What Students Produce	Success Criteria
Confidentiality	List 5 pieces of information that should be kept confidential	To gain an understanding of what should be treated as confidential and outline Data Protection Act 1998	Data protection Confidentiality Policy Procedures Compliance	A piece of writing outlining the importance of confidentiality and how non-compliance can affect businesses A short policy and corresponding procedure A short presentation outlining the Data Protection Act	Completion of written work Presenting to peers
Effective Teamwork		To introduce the concept of effective teamwork and how it links to customer service			

You and the World of Work

Traineeship					
You and the World of Work					
Lesson	Learning Objectives	Outline of Lesson	Keywords	What Students Produce	Success Criteria
British Values and Radicalisation	List 4 British values as defined by the UK government	To introduce British values and how we benefit from them	British values Radicalisation Extremism	Some research on extremist groups and historical cases	Completion and pass of Prevent training assessment
Global Citizenship	List 4 of the UN sustainable development goals List 3 extremist groups Identify 2 reasons why someone may be vulnerable to radicalisation	To introduce radicalisation and how you might identify a person vulnerable to radicalisation How to report suspected radicalisation Take Prevent test	Prevent United Nations Global citizenship Sustainable development Goals	A plan on how individuals can contribute to the UN SDGs	Be able to discuss the UN SDGs and how to contribute to the wider world
Arranging and Attending Meetings	To explain 4 formal meeting terms and attend and record a meeting with peers	Understand how to behave in formal meetings and together with some terminology	Quorum Minutes Motion Agenda	A set of minutes from their formal meeting	Production of a set of minutes

You and the World of Work

Traineeship					
You and the World of Work					
Lesson	Learning Objectives	Outline of Lesson	Keywords	What Students Produce	Success Criteria
Micro Teach	Plan and deliver a 15 minute microteach on a subject trainees care about	To create and deliver a short lesson on a subject they care about	Planning Content Learning outcomes Interactive	A lesson planned with interactive activities to support and reinforce learning	To be able to measure the learning outcomes for their lesson
Decision Making	To explain the 7-step decision-making model and work through decision-making exercises	To explore the decision-making process and how different decisions relate to different aspects of life	Pros and cons Conscious and unconscious decisions Open and closed questions	Contribute to group discussions about decision making	Explain their thought process for decision-making exercise

Traineeship

You and the World of Work

Lesson	Learning Objectives	Outline of Lesson	Keywords	What Students Produce	Success Criteria
Business Travel Task	To organise a business trip for a party of 4 and create a travel itinerary for each	Look at how business travel works and what should be considered to enable travel to be organised cost-effectively taking individual needs into account	Individual needs Itinerary	A detailed costing spreadsheet of the entire business trip A detailed Itinerary or travel plan for each person going on the trip	To be able to show a record of costings and remain within budget whilst meeting the needs of all travellers
Planning a Recruitment Event	Identify potential pipeline for recruiting new students Choose a suitable venue taking into consideration transport links and accessibility Create marketing materials to advertise your event Cost the event	To plan an event in pairs to encourage creativity and working collaboratively To be mindful of equality and diversity, and accessibility of the venue and what you are recruiting for	Pipeline Accessibility Marketing materials	A presentation of their ideas and costings for peer assessment	Complete and deliver presentation on time and receive positive feedback from peers

Traineeship

You and the World of Work

Lesson	Learning Objectives	Outline of Lesson	Keywords	What Students Produce	Success Criteria
Motivation Money as a Motivator – Bonus versus Commission?	Research a motivation theory Motivate your colleagues Create a plan to improve communication Introduce the concept of ERR	To introduce motivational theories and why people work – we can link this back to life planning sessions To understand the importance of professional and accurate communication	Bonus Commission Theories Legislation Contracts Probationary period	A guide to creating professional email communications A presentation on a motivational theory and why students relate to it or how they feel about it	Demonstrating an understanding of motivation theories and being able to discuss how they feel about them and what they think the pros and cons are Creating a professional communication about emailing policy and what makes a professional email
Employment Rights and Responsibilities (ERR)	Research employment Legislation	Outline what should be included in employment contracts		Research notes for employment legislation	

Project Work

Traineeship					
Project Work					
Lesson	**Learning Objectives**	**Outline of Lesson**	**Keywords**	**What Students Produce**	**Success Criteria**
Planning an Assessment Session	To identify and plan 2 tasks to showcase candidate skills	To get groups to work collaboratively to plan an assessment day to recruit for a role	Group tasks Scheduling Organisation	An itinerary for their assessment sessions Planned tasks for candidates to undertake Interview preparation	To have a detailed plan of their assessment session and a list of who will do what
Conducting an Assessment Session	To implement the assessment session plan and select 1 successful candidate	To work as a group to successfully implement their assessment session plan	Group tasks Scheduling Organisation	Detailed notes for feedback to candidates on their performance and an offer to the successful candidate	To have selected a successful candidate and provided constructive feedback to colleagues to help them improve

Project Work

Traineeship					
Project Work					
Lesson	Learning Objectives	Outline of Lesson	Keywords	What Students Produce	Success Criteria
Outstanding Assessment Tasks and Functional Skills Testing	To complete or resubmit any outstanding Onefile tasks To sit any functional skills exams	Student to liaise with their trainer to plan the day's activities and FS tutor to facilitate FS exams		Complete assessment tasks to meet criteria	Complete assessment tasks to meet criteria
Customer Complaints	To create a grammatically correct written response to a letter of complaint	Introduce and gain an understanding of how to deal with complaints in a positive way, using the correct language	Apologise Ownership Outcome	A letter of apology taking ownership of the complaint, outlining the findings of their investigation and action taken to rectify the problem	To create a letter that strikes the proper tone and is grammatically correct

Traineeship

Project Work

Lesson	Learning Objectives	Outline of Lesson	Keywords	What Students Produce	Success Criteria
Final Day Round Up	To have completed all Onefile tasks in readiness for work experience To have taken part in final classroom review	To use the final day to complete any unfinished tasks, or tasks that have been marked and need amending To review performance and receive feedback before entering the workplace	Onefile Assessment Tasks Review Feedback	Completion of any unfinished Onefile tasks	To have all Onefile tasks completed and signed off by tutor

Five Year Goals

Now we are going to recognise our own skills, abilities and interests for career planning.

Remember Tony Robbins' message! Clarity is key and you need to be ready with an alternative if plan A and plan B don't work out.

So, to ensure you have thought about alternatives, create one main career pathway and two alternatives. Justify how they tie into your skills, abilities and interests.

Using the timeline plan, let's set ourselves some yearly goals, these could be personal or professional.

Use the timeline template below as your guide. You will see that it narrows from yearly to monthly to weekly.

For now let's do the next five years.

Step 1	Step 2	Step 3
Write Down Your *Annual* Goals To Get To Your Five Year Goal – Review Yearly	Write Down Your *Monthly* Goals Just For The Next Year – Review Monthly	Write Down Your *Daily* Goals Just For The Next Week – Review Daily
eg **Goal** *– By the end of year 1 I want to find a job as an office administrator*	*eg* **Goal** *– By the end of month 1 I want to have a CV which is tailored to suit office admin roles*	*eg* **Goal** *– By the end of day 1 I want to have looked up office admin and listed the required skills*
Justification *– Because I have IT skills, I'm organised and I like structure to my day*		

Remember to always use the **SMART** method when setting goals – **S**pecific – **M**easurable – **A**chievable – **R**ealistic – **T**imed

Name:

Ultimate Goal:

Year One	Year Two	Year Three	Year Four	Year Five
Goal	Goal	Goal	Goal	Goal
Justification	Justification	Justification	Justification	Justification

Contingencies – What if things go wrong? What could you do instead?

1	1	1	1	1
2	2	2	2	2

Month One		Month Two		Month Three		Month Four	
Goal		Goal		Goal		Goal	

Month Five		Month Six		Month Seven		Month Eight	
Goal		Goal		Goal		Goal	

Month Nine		Month Ten		Month Eleven		Month Twelve	
Goal		Goal		Goal		Goal	

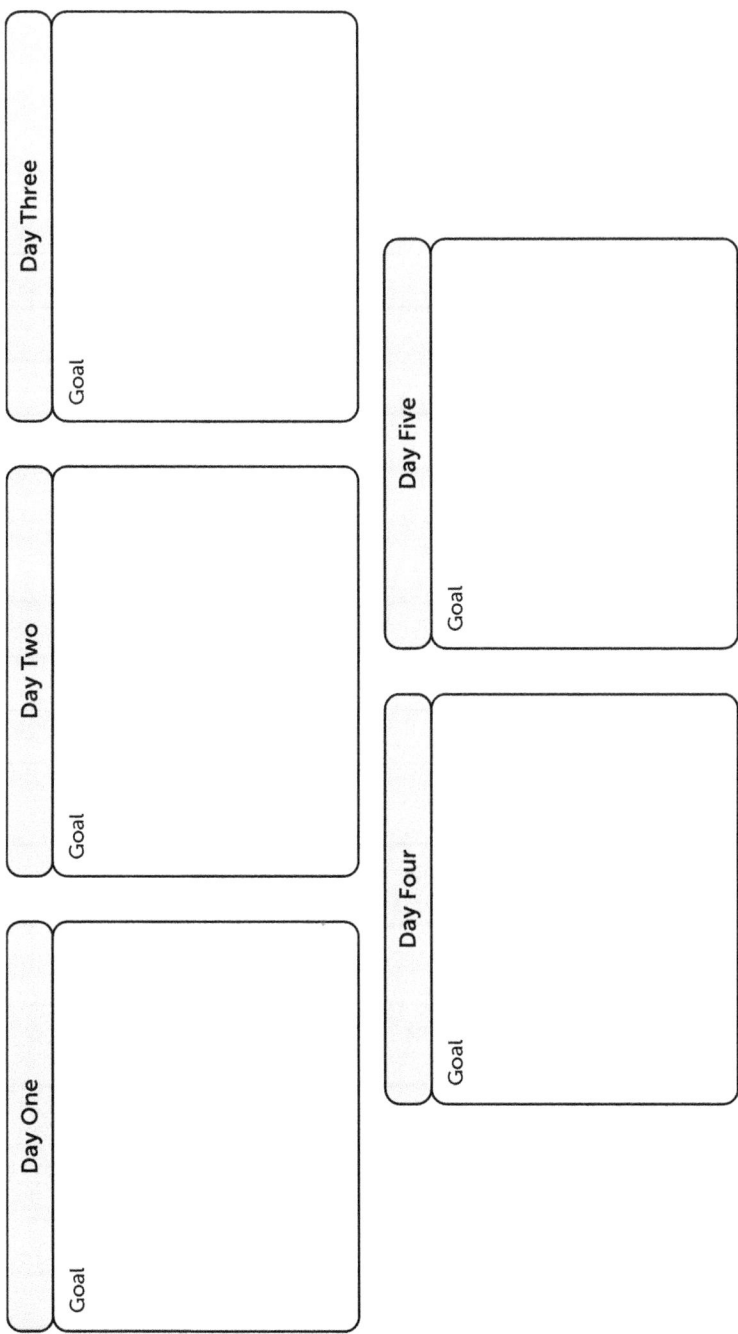

Day Three

Goal

Day Two

Goal

Day One

Goal

Day Five

Goal

Day Four

Goal

Life Plan Template

How old are you now?: ....

How old is your future self?:.............

	THESE ARE YOUR GOALS!
How happy are you?	
What do you look like?	
What are you wearing?	
How fit are you?	
What is your speech like?	
What impression do you make on people?	
What do people say about you?	
Where do you work?	
What's it like at work?	
What are your work colleagues like?	
How long have you been working there?	
What are your main responsibilities?	
What was the promotion path that got you there?	
What's the next career goal you're aiming for?	
Where do you live?	
Is it a house or a flat?	
What's it like inside?	

	THESE ARE YOUR GOALS!
How much did it cost you?	
Do you have a mortgage or do you rent?	
How long are you planning to stay there?	
What are your friends like?	
What do you do for hobbies?	
Are you married or with a partner?	
Do you have children?	
What is your partner like?	
What do they do for work?	
How do you travel? i.e. to work and back	
If it's a car - what car is it?	
How much did it cost you?	
Where did you buy it?	
Where do you go on holiday?	
How do you socialise?	
How do you help others?	
Rate your life out of 10	
10= The best it could possibly be 1= You are not very happy with your life	If it's not at least an 8 go back and change the answers! Find out how MiddletonMurray can help, by visiting www.middletonmurray.com

Life Plan

Remember Tony Robbins' message!

Clarity is key and you need to be ready with an alternative if plan A and plan B don't work out.

So, to ensure you have thought about alternatives create one main career pathway and two alternatives. Justify how they tie into your skills, abilities and interests.

Using the timeline plan let's set ourselves some yearly goals, these could be personal or professional.

Download the timeline template and use this as your guide. You will see that it narrows from yearly to monthly to weekly.

For now let's do the next five years.

You could create a flow chart like the template if you wish:

Add your justification to the chart to explain how this pathway ties into your skills, abilities and interests

OR

You create a written plan Starting with Year One.

Year One

Month 1

Month 2

Month 3 etc....

Helpful hints:

Always work backwards from your goal to where you are now. This may seem strange but it really does make planning easier.

The more a job suits your personality, the more enjoyable your working life will be.

OR

5 Year Goals

Plan A: Which broad area/sub-heading/type of company/type of job role?

Year 1:

Year 2:

Year 3:

Year 4:

Year 5:

Add your justification to Plan A to explain how this pathway ties into your skills, abilities and interests.

Plan B: Which broad area/sub-heading/type of company/type of job role?

Year 1:

Year 2:

Year 3:

Year 4:

Year 5:

Add your justification to Plan A to explain how this pathway ties into your skills, abilities and interests.

Plan C: Which broad area/sub-heading/type of company/type of job role?

Year 1:

Year 2:

Year 3:

Year 4:

Year 5:

Add your justification to Plan A to explain how this pathway ties into your skills, abilities and interests.

Tips Look at the following resources:

- Four broad areas worksheet
- Life plan template
- Niche template/Framework template (p156)
- Niche & USP template

NOTE When you have decided what sort of company/job role you wish to go into, go online to find examples of job descriptions so you understand the type of skills, abilities and experience they require!

Example

Plan A: Office & Technology (Business, Administration & Law) Recruitment company – job role: resourcer/recruitment consultant

Year 1:

Year 2:

Year 3:

Year 4:

Year 5:

Plan B: Leisure & Retail (Retail & Commercial Enterprise) Property services/estate agents – job role: administration or office junior and trainee negotiator

Year 1:

Year 2:

Year 3:

Year 4:

Year 5:

Niche template/sectors of work

1. **Firstly, list the things you most want in your job**

2. **Next, tick one of the four categories below which is most likely to enable you to achieve these things**

   Office and Technology Professionals

   Leisure and Retail Professionals

   Care and Education Professionals

   Construction and Infrastructure Professionals

3. **Now within that category, tick the box that best fulfils your criteria**

   OFFICE AND TECHNOLOGY
   Arts, media and publishing
   Business, administration and law
   Information and communication technology

   LEISURE AND RETAIL
   Leisure, travel and tourism
   Retail and commercial enterprise

   CARE AND EDUCATION
   Education and training
   Health, public services and care

   CONSTRUCTION AND INFRASTRUCTURE
   Construction, planning and the built environment
   Engineering and manufacturing technologies
   Agriculture, horticulture and animal care

Finally tick five categories that fulfil your criteria and then prioritise between 1 and 5

OFFICE AND TECHNOLOGY

ARTS MEDIA AND PUBLISHING
Advertising and Marketing Communications
Broadcast Production
Community Arts
Costume and Wardrobe
Craft and Technical Roles in Film and Television
Creative Craft Practitioner
Creative and Digital Media
Cultural and Heritage Venue Operations
Digital and Technology Degree Apprenticeship
Design
Junior Journalist (T)
Live Events and Promotions
Music Business
Photo Imaging
Sound Recording, Engineering and Studio Facilities
Technical Theatre Lighting, Sound and Stage

BUSINESS, ADMINISTRATION AND LAW
Accounting
Actuarial Technician (T)
Banking
Bookkeeping
Business and Administration
Business and Professional Administration
Business, Innovation and Growth
Contact Centre Operations
Enterprise
Financial Services Administrator (T)
Fundraising
Human Resources Management
Insurance

Legal Services
Management
Marketing
Payroll
Professional Services
Project Management
Providing Financial Services
Providing Mortgage Advice
Public Relations
Recruitment
Relationship Manager – Banking (T)
Sales and Telesales
Social Media and Digital Marketing
Volunteer Management

INFORMATION AND COMMUNICATION TECHNOLOGY

Information Security
IT Application Specialist
IT, Software, Web and Telecoms Professionals
Network Engineer (T)
Software Developer (T)

LEISURE AND RETAIL

LEISURE, TRAVEL AND TOURISM

Activity Leadership
Cabin Crew
Coaching
Golf Greenkeeper (T)
Instructing Exercise and Fitness
Leisure Management
Leisure Operations
Outdoor Programmes
Playwork
Spectator Safety
Sports Development

Sporting Excellence
Travel Services

RETAIL AND COMMERCIAL ENTERPRISE
Barbering
Beauty Therapy
Catering and Professional Chefs
Cleaning and Environmental Services
Commercial Moving
Energy Assessment and Advice
Express Logistics
Facilities Management
Fashion and Textiles
Funeral Operations and Services
Hairdressing
Hospitality
Hospitality Management
International Trade and Logistics
Licensed Hospitality
Logistics Operations
Mail and Package Distribution
Nail Services
Procurement
Property Services
Retail
Spa Therapy
Supply Chain Management
Trade Business Services
Vehicle Sales
Warehousing and Storage

CARE AND EDUCATION

EDUCATION AND TRAINING
Digital Learning Design
Learning and Development
Learning Support

Professional Development for
Work-Based Learning Practitioners
Supporting Teaching and Learning in Physical Education
Supporting Teaching and Learning in Schools

HEALTH, PUBLIC SERVICES AND CARE
Allied Health Profession Support
Assistant Practitioner
Care Leadership and Management
Children and Young People's Workforce
Clinical Healthcare Support
Community Safety
Court, Tribunal and Prosecution Administration
Custodial Care
Dental Laboratory Assistant (T)
Dental Nursing
Dental Practice Manager (T)
Dental Technician (T)
Emergency Case Assistance
Emergency Fire Services Operations
Employment Related Services
HM Forces
Health and Social Care
Healthcare Support Services
Housing
Intelligence Analysis
Legal Advice
Libraries, Archives, Records and Information Management
Services
Local Taxation and Benefits
Locksmithing
Maternity and Paediatric Support
Optical Retail
Pathology Support
Perioperative Support
Pharmacy Services

Policing
Providing Security Services
Security Systems
Witness Care
Youth Work

CONSTRUCTION AND INFRASTRUCTURE

CONSTRUCTION, PLANNING AND THE BUILT ENVIRONMENT

Building Energy Management Systems
Construction Building
Construction Civil Engineering
Construction Management
Construction Specialist
Construction Technical Supervision and Management
Plumbing and Heating
Property Maintenance (T)
Surveying

ENGINEERING AND MANUFACTURING TECHNOLOGIES

Aerospace Manufacturing Fitter (T)
Advanced Manufacturing Engineering
Aviation Operations on the Ground
Building Products Occupations
Building Services Engineering Technology
Bus and Coach Engineering and Maintenance
Ceramics Manufacturing Processes
Composite Engineering
Consumer Electrical and Electronic Products
Control/Technical Support Engineer
Domestic Heating
Driving Goods Vehicles
Electrical/Electronic Technical Support Engineer (T)
Electrotechnical

Engineering Construction
Engineering Environmental Technologies
Engineering Manufacture (Operator and Semi-Skilled)
Explosives Storage and Maintenance
Extractives and Mineral Processing Occupations
Food and Drink
Food and Drink Maintenance Engineer
Furniture, Furnishing and Interiors
Gas Industry
Glass Industry
Heating and Ventilation
Improving Operational Performance
Intelligence Operations
Interactive Design and Development
Jewellery, Silversmithing and Allied Trades
Laboratory and Science Technicians
Laboratory Technician (T)
Land-Based Engineering
Manufacturing Engineer (T)
Mechatronics Maintenance Technician (T)
Metal Processing
Mineral Products Technology
Multi-Skilled Vehicle Collision Repair
Nuclear Power Plant Operations
Nuclear Working
Operations and Quality Improvement
Passenger Carrying Vehicle Driving (Bus and Coach)
Polymer Processing Operations
Power Engineering
Power Industry
Power Network Craftsperson (T)
Print and Printed Packaging
Process Manufacturing
Product Design and Development Engineer (T)
Production of Coatings

Professional Aviation Pilot Practice
Rail Engineering – Overhead Line Construction
Rail Infrastructure Engineering
Rail Services
Rail Traction and Rolling Stock Engineering
Railway Engineering Design Technician (T)
Refrigeration and Air Conditioning
Science Manufacturing Technician (T)
Signmaking
Smart Meter Installations
Sustainable Resource Management
Traffic Office
Vehicle Restoration
Vehicle Body and Paint
Vehicle Fitting
Vehicle Maintenance and Repair
Vehicle Parts
Water Industry
Wood and Timber Processing and Merchant Industries

AGRICULTURE, HORTICULTURE AND ANIMAL CARE
Animal Care
Animal Technology
Blacksmithing
Environmental Conservation
Equine
Farriery
Fencing
Fish Husbandry
Floristry
Game and Wildlife Management
Horticulture
Maritime Occupations
Nursing Assistant in a Veterinary Environment
Veterinary Nursing

Purpose of a CV

There are thousands of articles and pieces of advice on what should go into a CV, how long it should be, how it should look and so on. I can give you my own view here and it is based on what I have seen work over the years. Before I show you a template, consider the purpose of the CV.

It is usually to secure you an interview, isn't it? Therefore you need to consider what will be most likely to achieve that. The answer is usually that your CV contains relevant experience and/or skills, that you have made some remarkable achievements, and that you appear to fit other criteria, which can vary hugely. Rightly or wrongly, employers do make decisions to interview based on a CV. Therefore it is vital that it contains all the information they need and it convinces them that they want to meet you.

Bearing in mind the purpose, we can now be clearer on the content.

Content of your CV

Summary, Skills and Qualifications, Work Experience, Key Achievements are the four most important headings. All the other information relating to hobbies, address, references etc do of course need to be there, but what you say under each of the above four headings will be the deciding factors.

Summary

This must explain in just a few sentences what you are seeking and why you would be of value to an employer in that field.

Skills and qualifications

A list of these in order of most recent first – with grades and with the place (school/college etc) where you took them. Skills don't have to be examinations by the way; they can include driving, languages, proficiency in a particular sport etc. These things are much better positioned here rather than in the hobbies section. List them in order of what is relevant to the job first. If you are not sure, always put the driving skill as the first one and the languages as the second, followed by the others.

Work experience and key achievements

These must be of relevance to the job you are interested in applying for. Therefore, if you are seeking a role in finance for example, you would want to put a key achievement that relates to that field. Your key achievements must be quantifiable. Rather than saying 'I spent four months helping to set up a new business' and just listing your tasks, you would say 'I spent four months helping to set up a new business during which time I implemented processes which saved one hour per day or saved £x per month'. Achievements are always best from an employer perspective if they can be linked in some way to the saving of time and money or the generation of revenue for their business.

Other points regarding content

Photo – This should be a professional headshot and I would suggest you put it at the top right of your CV. The same headshot should be used on your social media profiles rather than a variety of different ones.

Truthfulness – We have all heard cases where executives in high-powered jobs have suddenly lost their job because their CV was found to be untruthful. Please let that be lesson enough to you to ensure that your CV always contains the truth. If you wish you can leave out things that don't show you in the best light, but what you must not do is put anything in it that you cannot substantiate.

Do not make up skills or experience, do not exaggerate grades; all these things can and usually will be double-checked and you do not want to lose out on a job offer if things you have claimed turn out to be untruthful. One of the biggest concerns of an interviewer is that the person in front of them is trustworthy. If they find them not to be, they will most certainly not hire them – ever.

Gaps – It is inadvisable to have unexplained gaps in your CV. Readers will instantly be suspicious and wonder what you were doing during those gaps. It is best to be very honest about gaps in between jobs.

Length of your CV

There is much debate on this but I would suggest that you keep it to two pages. One page feels too short. More than two pages is definitely too long. So I would space it out with reasonably large print over two pages.

Many say that you need several versions of your CV but I would argue against that. You want to be absolutely happy with your CV and totally familiar with it when you are being interviewed.

Imagine if you are unsure what CV the interviewer is looking at for example! My recommendation is to have one version of your CV that is as excellent as possible. Then refine it as you go along – this keeps things simple for you and ensures that you put all your efforts into that one CV.

Template of a good CV is below but we update these regularly so for the very latest version go to www.1stjobseries.com

Mobile then **landline number**

Email: professional email address

Summary

4–5 sentences: A brief overview of your unique attributes (soft skills), background, summary of what you are doing at the moment and your future career aspirations (please see below as an example to use):

My current goal is to complete my Traineeship Programme and to progress on to a 12-month work placement and start my apprenticeship in Business and Administration.

Key skills

Examples of hard skills such as ICT, languages, problem solving, team working, subject knowledge etc in bullet points and then columns.

Training

Any training such as pre-apprenticeships, outdoor pursuits, first aid, computer training etc in chronological order. Example below:

- Six-Week Traineeship Programme at MiddletonMurray
- Workskills and Employability
- Customer Service
- 12 Steps to Recruitment

Also take this opportunity to share any additional achievements that you are proud of, eg Prince's Trust, Duke of Edinburgh Award.

Education and Qualifications

Sixth form, college, secondary school – dates started and finished and name of establishment, again in chronological order. Example below:

A levels

GCSEs

North West Kent College September 2011 – November 2011

Blackfen School for Girls September 2006 – June 2011

Work Experience and Key Achievements

A brief overview of your work experience including where it took place, duration and skills learned from the experience, again in chronological order. Example below:

Start Date – Present

MiddletonMurray – Six-Week Traineeship Programme

Training and work skills covered:

- Telephone answering workshop
- Different methods in applying for jobs
- How to construct a covering letter and professional CV
- Researching, creating and delivering PowerPoint presentations
- Public speaking
- Confidence building
- Following instructions
- ICT skills – use of Microsoft Word, PowerPoint and Outlook
- Working in a team and individually
- Working to deadlines and prioritising workloads

Employment History

If you do have any previous employment history then state it here starting with your most recent employment, state month and year, job role, activities/tasks. If not then leave this out.

Hobbies and Interests

Open with words like: In my spare time I enjoy...

References

Covering letter

Your covering letter is where you can distinguish yourself and bring out the points in your CV that are very relevant to the job you are applying for. It should expand on your personal summary in the CV.

Letters are now sent on a less and less frequent basis – so if you send one to a future employer it will make you stand out. You do however want to stand out for the right reasons! Therefore the quality of the letter must be exceptional. It goes without saying that the spelling and grammar must be perfect and so must the layout of the letter. Besides that, it is advisable that the quality of the paper and the envelope is good and that the letter is folded neatly into three. Use a first-class stamp and do make sure that you send it with a copy of your CV. This will impress the interviewer, and if they are torn between yourself and another candidate it may be enough to sway them over to you. So do take the time and effort to do this.

A template of a letter is below, however we update these regularly so for the most up to date version go to www.1stjobseries.com

Covering letter template

YOUR NAME
YOUR CONTACT DETAILS

TODAY'S DATE

EMPLOYER'S NAME
EMPLOYER'S TITLE
EMPLOYER'S ADDRESS

Dear (PERSON'S NAME OR DEAR SIR OR MADAM IF YOU ARE UNSURE)

RE: (name of position/vacancy – including vacancy number if applicable)

I am writing to apply for the position of (position title) at your company which was advertised in/on (name of newspaper/name of website etc.) on (date).

Having extensively researched your company's values and services, I was especially interested in (state the type of position and why you are interested in it and link this to your past experience and your key skills that are relevant to the job if you can).

I have enclosed my CV to support my application. It shows that I would bring important skills to the organisation including xxxx (list ones that are relevant to the job). At (school/previous job) I carried out duties such as xxxx. I am keen to develop my skills and always willing to undertake any training required to adapt to the needs of the business.

Add a paragraph to give the employer more information about how you match the job they are advertising. It is also good to show that you have some knowledge of the company with whom you are seeking employment and the role you are going for, so do a little research and use the information about the company which has been provided in the job description.

I would enjoy having the opportunity to talk with you more about this position and how I could use my skills to benefit your organisation and very much hope to hear from you. Thank you in advance for considering my application.

Yours sincerely (when you know the person's name, ie Dear Mr xxx)

Yours faithfully (when you don't know the person's name, ie Dear Sir/Madam)

Sign your name

PRINT YOUR NAME

Application forms

It is difficult to advise what to put in these as they are generally so diverse. There are, however, some general rules that apply to all:

- Perfect handwriting

- Exact extracts from your CV – certainly no contradictions

- Stick very strictly to the number of word rules, eg if they say 500 words give 498 words and not more but not much less

- In any sections where free format writing is requested make sure that every statement can be backed up by facts; for example, 'I am hard-working' needs to be supported by some facts to substantiate it – remember that all your competitors will say similar things, so yours needs to stand out with facts and proof rather than generalist statements

- Timeliness – ensure that the application form is delivered within the deadline

- Covering letter – if there is a covering letter, try to not duplicate what you have put into the application form but do refer to the various sections in the form

- Make sure you keep a copy!

- Make sure you complete all sections

Emails and voicemails

Your email address

You need a professional email address. Try to buy the domain of your name – in my case I have purchased www.angelamiddleton. com. If you cannot get that try using your middle name or a .co. uk domain or a .me domain. These are usually quite cheap to buy. Once you have them, set up your email address as your first name at the domain. For example, mine is angela@angelamiddleton. com. This not only looks professional but it is easy to remember and also it is future-proof, by which I mean that it does not have a year in it, nor does it have any reference to nicknames that I might want to shake off in a few years!

Your emails

Your emails should always be written professionally, as you would a letter, with Dear xxx at the beginning and Yours sincerely at the end. Full grammar rather than shorthand should be used. Also you need to have a signature at the bottom which is fixed and can contain a link to a video of you introducing yourself, your Twitter and LinkedIn pages, there can be a message in it and even a photo of you. At the very least it needs to contain your name and your telephone number so that people can contact you quickly. Your emails must add to your brand and strengthen it, they must not detract from it in any way, so be very careful with all emails that you send.

Your voicemails

Firstly please do consider the tone and sound of your voice. Most people when they are a bit nervous speak more quietly, more quickly and more high pitched. Therefore you should focus on ensuring that your voice is clear, loud (but not shouting!), slower than usual and deeper than usual. Check your voicemail message on your phone. Don't leave it as your phone provider's answerphone, but equally please do ensure that you have a well-worded and clear message for any callers. Write it down and rehearse it, and re-record it until you are happy with it.

Something like: "You have reached (your name). I am sorry I cannot take your call right now but please do leave a message and I will call you back as soon as possible. Many thanks for calling," is perfect. You must make sure you listen to your messages though!

Voicemail is not as popular with young people as it is with older people so you must get into the habit of listening. Not calling back the same day really does not leave a good impression, so aim to call back within the hour if you can.

Equally if you are calling someone about a job, do leave voicemail, don't just hang up. Something like: "Hello (their name), this is (your name) calling in connection with the letter I sent you about possible job opportunities. I would be very grateful if you or your assistant could call me back on (your number). Many thanks for your time." Once again, have this written down and rehearse it before you leave the message; if you are unhappy with it you can often re-record your message, so take advantage of that facility too if you need to. Obviously, do leave a number for them that you can always answer; don't leave a number that possibly other people might answer.

A pay-as-you-go phone to be used specifically for this purpose is a good idea if you don't already have a mobile phone.

Social media

Be careful!

If you are seeking your first job then this is the time to transform your social presence from just a social presence to a professional one. Social media can be a fantastic platform for you to let the world know about your skills and that you are seeking your first position. Do not be shy about this! The more people who know that you are looking, the more likely it is that you will receive help from someone who can influence your chances. Having said that, you do need to be careful and ensure that when people look at your online presence they are presented with a professional image. Often this step is missed by young people and can be their downfall with a job opportunity, and they may not even realise it.

Whenever I interview someone for a position I check out their online presence after the interview to check that it matches up to what they have said at interview. There has been more than one occasion where what I have been told does not match up with what I have seen on their Facebook for example and consequently they have not been offered the position. Don't let your online presence trip you up like this — instead let it become a tool that increases your chances of success!

Principally I am talking about LinkedIn, Twitter, Facebook and Instagram here (the latter less so). In just the same way as your CV needs to sell you, so do these profiles. Take a look at them at the moment, would you hire you based on what you see? If not, then do something about it well before you start sending out your applications and inviting people to find out about you.

Facebook

With your Facebook (even if you no longer use it very much) I would suggest this is reserved for your personal use and that you simply lock down all the privacy settings so that only your friends can see your content and not friends of friends or the public. Also I would suggest you audit your list of friends and remove anyone you don't know and trust; you just don't know who they know and who they could show your content to. Facebook changes its privacy settings often so this is something that you should do regularly.

One thing I would say however is that Facebook is a rich source of referrals if you ask for them. Update your status regularly about your job search, how you are getting on, keep on asking for more referrals. Sometimes people need to see this a number of times before they are called to action and, as we know, not everything you write is seen by everyone, so if you update at different times of day and night then it is more likely that all your friends will see this at some stage.

Your profile picture

Ensure that your profile picture is one that you would not be embarrassed for an employer to see. One of you achieving something would be great, but otherwise just a nice friendly headshot. Avoid any where you are out socially – keep those for within your Facebook. Don't wear sunglasses in it, no pouting or pulling faces, making signs with your hands etc, just a nice clear picture that looks like you!

LinkedIn

You may not have a LinkedIn profile as yet. LinkedIn is like Facebook for business people. Basically you connect with people and then they are known as first connections. Then all their connections are known as your second connections. Unless they lock those down, you can look at all their connections and invite them to connect too. You can search all your connections for key words, meaning you can use it to find out names of people who do particular types of jobs, for example.

In the same way, anyone on LinkedIn can search by key word, and employers and recruiters often do. You may come up in their search if you have the right key words that they are searching for in your profile. Also jobs are advertised on LinkedIn, and you can direct message your connections. There is a feed so you can see latest news about people's new jobs, their anniversaries of jobs, and of course their status. You can update your status as with Facebook, you can add photos and documents, as well as presentations etc. You can follow companies and you can join groups. For someone starting out in their career as well as building their career, it really is an important tool and is second only to your CV in demonstrating your skills experience.

It is very important that your LinkedIn profile reflects exactly what is on your CV, ie they must not clash. You can use some of the wording of your CV and build on it. You can attach your CV. On a daily basis spend some time on LinkedIn, adding your contacts that are already on your list and also reviewing and adding their contacts. You should make sure that you use key words in your profile that relate to the industry you want to get into, to maximise your chances of appearing if employers or recruiters are searching for people in your chosen industry.

Update your status daily with your progress on your job search; this will ensure that you keep on appearing on the news feed of your connections, and this in itself might achieve some job opportunities for you. Make sure your updates are placed at different times of day and night and also over the weekend; do maximise your chances of your updates being seen by as many of your connections as possible. Set up saved searches of jobs so they appear on your news feed. Join groups relevant to your industry. Follow companies that you would like to work for. All of this will help build your online presence and build your network for the future.

Go to www.linkedin.com and search for Angela Middleton to see my example profile.

Twitter

As with Facebook, you may already have a private Twitter account that you use to communicate with followers and those that you follow. Once again, look at this as if you were a future employer. What does it show and say about you? If there is anything that you wouldn't want an employer to see about you, then shut it down and set yourself up a more professional one. Certainly if the Twitter handle that you have is not professional sounding, then set up a new one. As I have already stated, Twitter is a great place to build your audience of employers that might hire you, and it is also a great place to display your ever building knowledge of the industry by tweeting new things you have discovered or heard that day and by updating people on your job search. As with LinkedIn, the more people who see you are searching, the better.

On your Twitter profile do ensure you leave your email address and a summary about the type of career you are seeking to build, also put a link on there to your LinkedIn profile. Remember that when you update status on LinkedIn you have an option for it to update Twitter automatically too. I would suggest you switch off that option due to the 140 word limit on Twitter constraining what you want to say on LinkedIn, and just do separate updates on each. Never use this Twitter account for comments regarding social life; you are building a professional profile here so don't let it slip. Also do retweet things you have found out or think are good.

Be generous with what you share, and support and encourage those you follow rather than just talking about yourself. This will help you engage with more followers.

Go to www.twitter.com and search for Angela Middleton to see an example profile.

Instagram

Instagram is becoming ever more popular for business so you will be able to message businesses to see if opportunities are there. If you have an Instagram channel with followers then, as with Facebook, do make sure that it is private, and secondly do announce to your followers that you are seeking a new role. Once again, you may well find that they know someone who can advise you or refer you.

Video (YouTube)

Producing a video of yourself speaking to the camera is still an unusual way of promoting yourself but can be very impactful, and you can set up your own YouTube channel using your name to display it on.

We have prepared videos for several young people we have helped.

These can be done very simply using your mobile phone. They should normally just be a headshot position and the best ones will show you in business dress explaining what sort of position you are seeking and why an employer should hire you. They really shouldn't be longer than a minute.

The great thing about this type of video is that you can rehearse it as many times as you wish until it's perfect and then you can add it to your profile, meaning employers and recruiters can get to see you before they invite you for interview.

Bear in mind that research shows that employers make their hiring decisions based on only 10% of what you say and the rest is about how you appear and how you say things (stats mention ability to hold eye contact, personal appearance, strength of handshake as all being extremely influential on the decision). Therefore, if they like what they see and hear they might then invite you for interview, even if what they see on your CV is not exactly what they were looking for. Of course you do run the risk with this that they don't like what they see and hear and so it causes them not to invite you for interview – but then in that case you would have been unsuccessful at interview anyway so it is best to find out beforehand and not waste your time.

Interview questions to practise

Here are some questions for you to ask but you can find loads more at www.1stjobseries.com

THE COMPANY

1. What is it about the company that makes people want to stay/made you join and stay?

2. How does the company encourage a coming together of staff through activities?

3. What is the company renowned for within the industry?

4. What position does the company hold in the marketplace?

5. What are the company's plans for the future?

6. What is the company's current annual growth rate?

7. How has your recent merger/takeover altered the company if at all?

8. How many offices are there?

THE DEPARTMENT

1. What exactly does the department do in terms of the overall company?

2. What are the department's plans for expansion?

3. What are the ages of the people in the department? What age group are the other members of the department?

4. What is/are the personality/ies of the people I would be working for/with?

5. How closely does this department work with other areas of the company?

6. How does this department compare in size to others within the organisation?

7. To what extent do you encourage staff to interact between departments?

TRAINING AND APPRAISAL

1. What sort of training is offered to staff within the department?

2. Is training provided in-house or are courses held externally?

3. What training facilities are available within the department/company?

4. What encouragement is given to further study?

5. How often do you hold meetings to assess the skills/abilities/progress of staff?

6. Who would I talk to about my progress and how often would this take place?

THE JOB

1. How would you describe a typical day for the person doing this job?

2. What would I have to do for you to feel I had done a really good job?

3. What systems do you use?

4. Who is doing the job at the moment?

5. What sort of handover will there be with the person who is currently doing this job?

6. Why did the last person leave? Were they with you for a long time?

7. What percentage of my job would be typing and what percentage would be administration?

8. You have asked for someone with good PowerPoint/Excel skills. How big a part does this play in the role? To what extent would I use my PowerPoint/Excel skills?

9. What type of person are you looking for to fill this role?

10. What competencies are you looking for the new person to have?

11. Who would I be reporting to?

12. How long has the person I will be working for been here?

13. How long have you been here?

14. How long would you expect a person to stay in this role?

15. Will there be the opportunity to become involved and work on my own initiative?

16. If I am keen to develop the role what would you like done?

PROSPECTS

1. What structures are in place for career development?

2. What are the promotional prospects? What prospects are there for career progression?

3. If I begin as a junior now, where could I hope to be within the company in 5/10 years' time?

4. How do you encourage staff to progress within the company?

5. How do you see this role developing?

6. What are the long-term development opportunities for this role?

7. What is the process for advertising jobs internally?

INTERVIEW PROCESS

1. When can I look around the department where I would be working?

2. When do you think you will decide on your shortlist for second interviews?

3. How many more people do you expect to interview for this position?

4. When do you expect to be able to make a decision?

SPECIAL QUESTIONS ON INTERVIEW PROCESS

1. When are you looking to take someone on board?

2. If you were interested in my application, when is the position to start? When are you looking for the selected candidate to start?

3. What is the next step from here?

4. What further interviews are proposed for someone successful at this stage?

Questions you might be asked

This depends on the job you are being interviewed for. Broadly speaking they fall into the following categories:

Competency questions

These are questions relating to the industry and job itself, or to other areas, such as hobbies. You will only be asked these if you have claimed to have experience, knowledge and skills, so please do ensure that you only say you have experience, knowledge or skills that you truly do. Don't exaggerate, otherwise the interview is the place where you will be found out! I once wrote on my CV that I enjoyed current affairs and was asked by the interviewer what I thought of the devolution of Scotland and the Corrie bill on abortion, which were apparently in the news that week. I knew nothing of either and consequently failed the interview, so do beware!

Template competency questions at www.1stjobseries.com

Scenario questions

These are questions asking you to describe what you would do in a certain situation. They are expecting you to draw on expertise and knowledge, although I always think these types of questions are also a good judge of someone's imagination. It is very difficult to advise what these questions might be, but it could include things like 'how would you deal with a situation where you were in conflict with your colleague?' These are very difficult questions to know how to respond to and the trick is to consider how the employer might want you to behave in that situation and then respond accordingly. Remember that the employer has a whole series of concerns that they want to eliminate. They don't want to hire those who might cause conflict, go sick, upset others, be lazy, not grasp things quickly enough etc, so make sure that these questions give you a chance to describe how you would be just the opposite.

Questions about you

Obviously you know yourself well and so you will know everything about yourself there is to know. Nevertheless, if you are asked to tell the employer about yourself you should still have your elevator pitch ready.

Elevator pitch: (when asked: "Tell me about yourself ")

Starting point: You need to have a start/beginning, state your name, age, where you live, which school you attended and what you achieved there by telling them how many GCSEs you gained, and if you have grades A-C then highlight the key subjects such as English, maths and ICT. Talk about any additional activities you did, such as part of the school football team or football team outside of school, other sporting activities eg the Duke of Edinburgh Award. Again you are thinking about telling them your USPs: unique selling points!

Middle point: You then need to explain what you did next after leaving school, so talk about your unpaid work experience or employment, what skills and duties you performed while there, and that you can bring these skills to your next job.

Ending point: Now tell them what you as a person can offer that employer, how you can benefit or add value to their company, why you are right for their role. Finish off by thanking them for listening.

Template elevator pitch at www.1stjobseries.com

Podcast Resources on iTunes – Angela Middleton's 'iwant2ba'

An A-Z of interviews with successful people in all types of careers explaining how they got there and how you can too!

PODCAST DASHBOARD

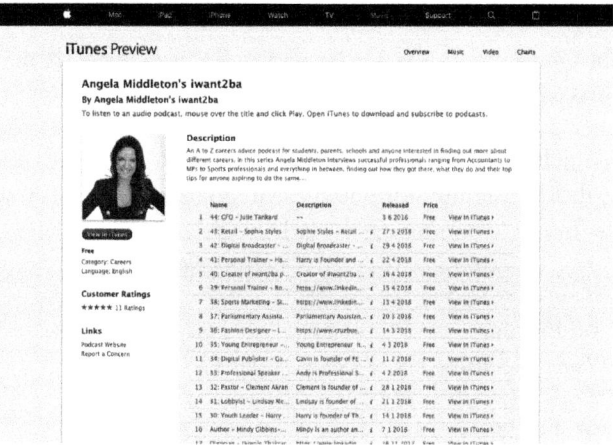

www.1stjobseries.com resources

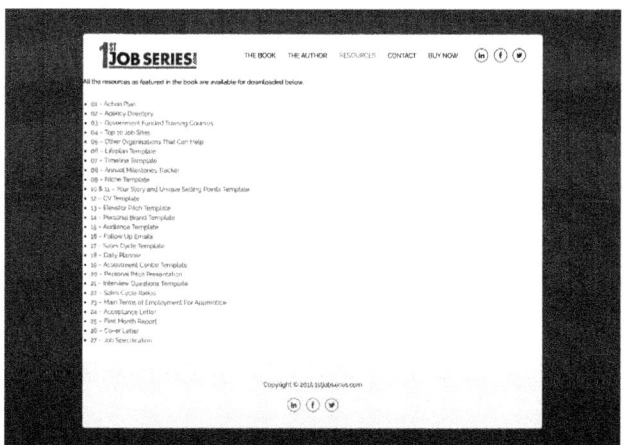

Templates mentioned in the book and tons of additional resources

Video resources all available on YouTube

Limitless Vlog Episode 1
https://www.youtube.com/watch?v=-rXENdYtwn4

Digital Marketing Apprenticeships
https://www.youtube.com/watch?v=xYwXGdlcvYE

Student Goals – and how we helped students achieve them!
https://www.youtube.com/watch?v=dEsoS-5KqMM

Meet Angelo, our new Data & Systems Apprentice! Find out how setting short-, medium- and long-term goals has helped Angelo take the first steps on his career ladder with MiddletonMurray.
https://www.youtube.com/watch?v=p5SA6Hb55fY

iwant2ba Promo
https://www.youtube.com/watch?v=vttOri_jvz4

iwant2ba Promo (2)
https://www.youtube.com/watch?v=vnkSjcFwBT4

Made in Kent
https://www.youtube.com/watch?v=hK-pWvCm_sQ

Angela joined the Sky News team to discuss GCSE Results 2017 and the virtues of apprenticeships and vocational careers
https://www.youtube.com/watch?v=4ncyu-O8GPs&t=310s

Apprenticeship Levy
https://www.youtube.com/watch?v=VqXy5MAA1nQ&t=41s

BBC *Inside Out*
https://www.youtube.com/watch?v=dzCF8WkkNSk

Apprentice of the Month

Our Apprentice of the Month scheme was created in 2013 to celebrate and encourage outstanding achievement. In addition it has been a UK-wide challenge for the apprenticeship qualification to have the same recognition as its equivalent academic qualifications and we felt that a monthly award scheme of this nature would help address this.

We appointed a judging panel consisting of eminent business people as well as successful apprentices who kindly give their time each month to review the nominations and select the winner. Each month we ask our apprenticeship tutors to review the performance of their virtual cohorts (each tutor has between 30 and 40 apprentices allocated to a similar number of employers) and submit their nomination for Apprentice of the Month. They then engage with both the employer and the nominated apprentice to put together a nomination justification. In addition our marketing team interview the employer, apprentice and tutor to create a visual nomination too. The nominations are submitted to the judging panel and a decision is made. Very often it is a close call! Critieria are not preset and so very often the judges are presented with fantastic nominations where apprentices have excelled for different reasons. It is difficult to select in these circumstances.

Once the winner is decided upon, we create the award trophy, purchase a gift and liaise with the employer to organise the surprise announcement to the apprentice. This usually takes place in the workplace and it's a wonderful occasion, often leaving the apprentice totally surprised and overwhelmed. The pictures and films from the day are then distributed widely on social media and it is therefore regarded as a huge accolade for all concerned. Our intention this year is to appoint an Apprentice of the Year from all 12 monthly winners, follow @middletonmurray on all social platforms to find out more!

Apprenticeships for school leavers are just the start. With changes in government focus on adult skills and the introduction of an apprenticeship levy for large companies, every member of the UK workforce is now eligible for an apprenticeship. To this end, we have an MP enrolled as an apprentice, several engineers, many graduates, and people who are over 50, to name just a few examples. Employers are now able to design their own apprenticeships which can go up to degree level and hence we see a number of professionals who want to scale the career ladder opting for an apprenticeship within their existing role.

YourBodyMeansBusiness

In addition, we offer online courses such as our new YourBodyMeansBusiness course which offers people wanting to take their career to the next level an holistic approach focusing not just on skills and business strategies, but also mind and body for optimal performance. Our premise is that learning never stops and that to excel one needs to address all the aspects of performance.

Follow me on all social media platforms @angelamiddleton to see more examples – all offered under our #LIMITLESS brand.

Example school success stories

Careers advice pilot scheme success at Cleeve Park

As part of MiddletonMurray's service for schools, colleges, universities and local authorities, MiddletonMurray staff, along with guest presenters Steve Rudd of ITRM and Chris Smith, a digital marketing specialist, recently took part in a highly successful two-day Careers Advice and Industry Sector Awareness pilot programme at Cleeve Park School in Sidcup, Kent.

Cleeve Park commissioned MiddletonMurray to undertake the pilot programme to bring the company's expertise into the school to assist with building their year 11 students' awareness of career opportunities and pathways into the various industry sectors.

Talking about the two-day project, Jenni Tyler-Maher of Cleeve Park School said: "The Careers Advice and Industry Sector pilot project with MiddletonMurray gave the students at Cleeve Park access to a range of employment opportunities and opened their minds to new avenues of careers that were previously unknown to them."

Jenni continued: "Over the two days, MiddletonMurray staff helped students prepare CVs and job applications, provided tips on interview techniques, and made presentations on a range of subjects including: Business & Finance, Hospitality, Technology, Luxury Retail and Construction."

The feedback from the Cleeve Park year 11 students was extremely positive, with 89% of the students believing that the Careers Advice and Industry Sector programme was a beneficial experience. 93% felt that the presentations were useful, whilst 94% found the speakers 'engaging' and 'inspirational'. Comments from the students included: "Today has helped me understand how to write my CV and to prepare"; "I found the tips about job interviews very useful"; and "It gave me good CV writing skills and an insight into future careers."

MiddletonMurray's Associate Director Jenny Shepherd, who co-ordinated the two days, said: "My colleagues and I enjoyed our time at Cleeve Park School and we were very pleased by how receptive the students were and by how supportive everyone at the school was in helping to make our Careers Advice and Industry Sector Awareness pilot programme such a success. We look forward to developing our relationship further with Cleeve Park School over the coming months."

About The Author

Angela grew up in south-east London and like many children received limited careers advice. She spent 20 years in corporate life working for BP Oil and Barclays before starting her first careers related business in 2002.

Angela has worked as a judge on Richard Branson's Voom panel – advising Richard on the best SMEs to invest in. She is also a regular contributor to public policy – including providing evidence on a number of Parliamentary Committees.

Her business interests are all accumulated under the 'Limitless' brand and include leading traineeship and apprenticeship company MiddletonMurray and the online careers and fitness coaching programme YourBodyMeansBusiness.com.

In June 2018 Angela launched her Limitless manifesto in the House of Commons where she announced that careers advice should be free and accessible to all. Her free podcast series IWant2BA accessible on iTunes is first of its kind in the UK. Angela published her first book *How to Get Your First Job and Build The Career You Want* in June 2015. This new book is the second in her First Job series.

Notes:

Notes:

_____

_____

_____

_____

_____

_____

_____

_____

_____

_____

_____

_____

_____

_____

_____

_____

Notes:

Notes:

Notes:

Notes: